THE LAST
BELIEVER

THE LAST BELIEVER
ESCAPING A CONDITIONED WORLD

By Daniel Senga

The Last Believer: Escaping a Conditioned World
English USA
Copyright © Daniel Senga 2016

ISBN-10: 0-9981860-0-7
ISBN-13: 978-0-9981860-0-9

First Edition

All rights reserved. No part of this publication may be reproduced, distributed, or transmitted in any form or by any means, including photocopying, recording, or other electronic or mechanical methods, without the prior written permission of the publisher, except in the case of brief quotations embodied in critical reviews and certain other noncommercial uses permitted by copyright law. For permission requests, write to the publisher, addressed "Attention: Permissions Coordinator," to the email address below.

Unless otherwise indicated, all Scripture quotations are taken from the New King James Version®. Copyright © 1982 by Thomas Nelson. Used by permission. All rights reserved. Nashville, Tennessee, U.S.A.

Edited by Greg Baker
Book cover designed by Lisa Hainline
Book interior designed by www.spbookdesign.com

Printed by IngramSpark/Lightning Source.

Published by: Jarme

Meditation Garden
contact@ziongarden.org
www.jarme.org

DEDICATION

I dedicate this book to those who love the Kingdom of God and who are looking forward to its coming and to those who still have faith in our Lord Jesus Christ and believe that the Bible is the Word of the living God.

CONTENTS

Introduction 9

UNIT 1: UNDERSTANDING SATAN'S PLAN............... 15

1. Humanity's Identity Crisis: Trinity vs. Animal 17
The New Identity 18
Spirit or Body?...........................22

2. The Worship Battle........................ 29
The Priority List........................... 31
Man's Spirit Is the Human Connection to
   God's Realm 37

3. The Freedom Campaign.....................45
The Government Agenda: Democracy....... 47
The Economic Agenda: Capitalism 49
The Family Agenda 50
What Really Happens 53
Divine Safeguards.........................55

UNIT 2: CONDITIONING IN THREE MAJOR PHASES.......... 67

4. Age of Expression: Make Them Believe
the Illusion 69
The Shadow of Reality......................71
Satan's Strategy 78

5. Age of Senses: Make Them Believe
It's All about Feelings 93
Why Age of "Senses"?......................95
Cultivation: Social Behavior Engineering......97

6. Age of the Gods: Make Them Believe
They Are Gods............................109

After the Fall 110
  How We Got Here 111
  Becoming Gods..............................118
  Living Conditions...........................119
  Spiritual and Philosophical Mind-set 120

UNIT 3: WHAT HAPPENS IN THE END? 123

7. Clueless: How to Believe in Jesus and End Up in Hell...............................125
  The "Thorns Effect": Spiritual Retardation .. 126
  Unable to Submit to Anyone and God 128
  Double Agent Satan 130
  World Government 133
  Controlling the World Wealth 134
  Destroying Family 135
  A Feminist Approach to the Word of God ...137

8. The Five Gates of Heaven: True Salvation 141
  Decoy Salvation.............................141
  Decoy Forgiveness 142
  Induced Guilt-Resistant.....................143
  Salvation 145

INTRODUCTION

One day Satan came up with the greatest scheme the universe has ever known—a masterpiece and proof of his great seductive prowess. He envisioned the destruction of humanity and all that has been given to it. The sin of Adam and Eve was just the tip of the iceberg. What followed after the introduction of sin is an extraordinary development that consumed the human essence from the outside and moved slowly into its core. Over its course, humanity will undergo a social, spiritual, and mental transformation as a result of the evolution of sin from inception to maturity.

In the end, two things will happen. On the one hand, multitudes will be redeemed through the sacrifice of the Son of God. On the other hand, the rest of the world will be conditioned toward unbelief. In other words, they will be programmed to become incapable of faith.

This book lays out how sin has evolved through time and space. It discusses the strategies and tools Satan uses to transform thousands and maybe millions of people into souls that can never turn to God and be saved, just like children who have gone so far and can no longer find their way back home. I describe this progression, highlighting major changes throughout the history of humanity, including not only past and current transformations, but also a prophetic perspective on future transformations.

The fall of Adam and Eve was the starting point of a much bigger satanic plan. Its cleverness, subtleness, and almost undetectable deceitfulness makes this plan perfect for social behavior transformation. Its unavoidability makes it look like normal social change instead of systematic engineering of culture and human behavior. It spares no social group, no race, no religion, and no philosophy. This plan allows Satan to gain the ability to dictate:

- What clothes people wear
- What food they eat
- Which politician they vote for
- What sermon they listen to

- What message the media conveys
- What is important in life
- What is right
- What is wrong
- And many other things I can't fit on this list

Satan's plan consists of changing man so that he lives like other animals, indefinitely competing for survival. Satan envisions a world where man is no longer identified as spirit, soul, and body, but a world where self is equivalent to only the body (flesh), a new man whose body dominates the spirit and the soul. With the help of the media and scientific claims, many believe that life has no meaning.

The body's domination of spirit and soul does not sound like such an awful thing upon first glance. However, it is the key to everything Satan wants to achieve. Many have written to explain what the spirit, soul, and body are, but it seems very few have focused on the roles they play.

To understand how sin evolves in the life of a person, one must understand how the roles of the spirit, soul, and body have evolved across time and how humanity has changed from its condition before the Fall. Therefore, in this book, we discuss how the spirit, soul, and body are supposed to work together as well as how demonic activities strive to disrupt their original order so that they serve a different purpose than God's original intent.

Those who will be born during the last moments of the world are raised, taught, and acculturated to unbelief. Their environment and way of life will be structured in such a way that there can only be one outcome: the willful embracement of the Antichrist spirit. I am not speaking of the incarnation of Satan who rises to become the world leader, but an overall spirit of Antichrist that controls a person's life, desires, ambitions, and beliefs. When this spirit has conquered enough souls, almost every man, woman, and child who lives on the surface of earth will become a part of a coalition against religion, faith, and God.

The most intriguing aspect of the evolution of sin is how much the Bible reveals about its progression. God, being omniscient, has supernaturally enabled His servants to document thousands of years of predictions that give shocking details from the day sin entered humanity to the day Christ will proclaim His eternal kingdom on Mount Zion.

However, Satan, knowing human nature too well, has set his mind to seduce the greatest number of people possible. In the end, those who do not receive the Spirit of life through Christ will have been conditioned to have no interest in knowing God. They are deceived into advancing Satan's plan. In fact, many of those who claim to serve Christ find themselves working against the Christ they are trying to serve.

Nevertheless, at that time, a great number will be marked by the Spirit of the living God so that when Satan employs his most effective acculturation techniques, their redeemed spirits will remain uncorrupted by the powers of darkness. Although they will struggle in their walk with God, their hearts will have reached a place of no return in the Lord's hands. No matter how compromised, sexualized, and ungodly the world becomes, they will look at it through the eyes of God, and their very presence in the world becomes a message of judgment. They will be a threat to the Antichrist's developing government.

While most religions will collapse around the world, they will grow stronger, because they are preparing themselves to be supernaturally taken from the world. These believers are known biblically as the saints of the harvest hour. Jesus Christ promised them in Matthew 13:24-29 and 13:41-43 that He *"will send out his angels"* at the harvest to separate those who fear God from those who have been deceived to join Satan's rebels.

The world has rejected values, such as faith, honor, and family, and has embraced immorality to gain pleasure. The pursuit of happiness has become the creed by which the majority now live by. In other words, the philosophy states that the pathway to one's envisioned happiness must be protected at all cost. Anything or anyone that gets in its way must be crushed.

However, the last believers will pursue something different. The thickening darkness in the world leads them to despise the ways of the world and, most importantly, ignites passion for the Kingdom of God. While many who claim to be believers will dilute God's principles to justify why they are increasingly becoming "*lovers of pleasure rather than lovers of God*" (2 Timothy 3:4), the last believer longs for the Kingdom of God and cannot wait for the promise of the rapture to be fulfilled.

During the last generations, Satan will find it difficult to work with those who are raised as believers. Even if they walk away from their faith, aspects of God's principles still linger in their hearts. Most prodigal sons are likely to return home in time. Therefore, mere rebellion against God as a goal becomes inefficient for Satan. Now he aims for people to be raised as complete rebels who are incapable of faith.

How then does he raise a generation of people who are incapable of faith? Does he succeed? What happens to the last generation of believers? This book will seek to answer these questions.

UNIT 1

UNDERSTANDING SATAN'S PLAN

CHAPTER 1

HUMANITY'S IDENTITY CRISIS

TRINITY VS. ANIMAL

THE FIRST STEP in Satan's plan to raise a generation of faithlessness involves changing the traditional understanding of human nature. Because many still believe that a human being is comprised of spirit, soul, and body, Satan is not able to launch a full-scale rebellion against God. Satan's attempts generally fail because, regardless of how they live their natural lives, people still fear the possibility that, one day in the afterlife, they may be held accountable for how they lived their natural lives.

Satan doesn't want people to believe in life beyond death, because it gives them an incentive to seek God.

He knows that the only way to overcome this obstacle is to create a human identity crisis that ultimately convinces society that the spiritual realm does not exist.

THE NEW IDENTITY

To accomplish his goal, Satan deceives humanity into questioning its own identity. The Word of God clearly reveals that a human being is made of a spirit, a soul, and a body. However, Satan is trying to initiate an identity crisis in such a way that human society undergoes a radical transformation. The key to his plan is to plant the idea that there is nothing more to a human being than the physical body. If successful, he will cause the modern world to endorse the psychological and spiritual changes that will make the rise of the Antichrist possible.

When humanity identifies itself as only a physical body, natural life—the least valuable aspect of human life—becomes the most valuable in the eyes of men. Because there is no other life to look forward to after death, humans work hard to protect a fragile and easily lost life. They work hard to improve life, yet their advances to achieve this quality of life ultimately destroys not only human life itself, but also the planet that supports it.

The loss of a true, spiritual identity causes the majority of the world to focus on the pursuit of happiness as its ultimate goal. Because of that, people spend a lot of time and energy trying to satisfy insatiable longings and desires. However, it has always been evident that finding such fulfillment comes at a very high cost. What people trade for temporary pleasures is immeasurable, and they do so because Satan has convinced them that there is only one life—you either enjoy it or it is wasted.

The loss of this true identity creates accessory lives that we trade valuable things for. Other than being alive, where does the notion of "my life" come from? What do people mean when they say, "This is my life" or "What do you want to do with your life?" The concept of "my life" is an accessory to life that was introduced into language as a result of a shift in human perception of our identity, specifically going from a spiritual being to just a physical being. In other words, the notion of "my life" gains weight when people cease to perceive themselves as primarily spiritual beings and increasingly see themselves as only natural. This notion creates a market where Satan can facilitate the trade of real life substances, such as faith, love, and compassion, for human conceptualized substances of life, such as a comfortable home, a career, and social status.

For instance, many believers have made divorce an acceptable option to solve marriage problems because of the "my life" concept. Although we may claim that we are spiritual people, subconsciously we identify life as physical and therefore cater to our bodies. And once believers get into that frame of mind, they live in the same fears that nonbelievers live in. The only difference is how we vocalize our excuses. For example, when you ask believers why they divorced, you often hear:

- "I felt like God could use my life for more."
- "I was going to lose my life."
- "My life was falling apart before my eyes."

All these statements about life have, in fact, nothing to do with the life Jesus Christ talks about when He stated in John 13:6 that *"I am the way, the truth, and the **life**. No one comes to the Father except through Me"* (emphasis added). The "life" from the phrase "my life" is a set of human desires and longings we try to satisfy. This notion of life in a worldly sense is purely associated with the physical body or our natural lives. However, the life Christ refers to is the true life that encompasses the entire being (spirit, body, and soul). This spiritual life exists to fulfill God's purpose, but when life is perceived as the "my life," then it exists to satisfy a list of human desires and longings or it is perceived as wasted.

In the life of a child of God, it is never a question whether life will be spent well or wasted; instead, it is a question whether God's purpose is fulfilled or not. The only way people would think in terms of fulfilling God's will is if they know and identify themselves as spiritual beings. The majority of us only claim to be spiritual, but only few actually perceive themselves as spiritual beings. Loss of the correct identity triggers erroneous ideas about life. Indeed, because of these new notions regarding life, divorce seems like a small price to pay in order to put a few check marks in the "my life" column of desires and ambitions.

This is how far humans can fall by just exalting the physical body above the spirit. When the body is exalted above the spirit, believers do spiritual things to invest in natural things and they do natural things thinking that they are investing in spiritual things. For instance, they may go to church and think that by doing so they are seeking God, but their real motive of the heart is the hope God will invest in their earthly lives. Going back to divorce, despite how clear Scripture is on the topic, a believer whose spiritual identity has become a natural identity may even think that a divorce will allow them to grow spiritually. Satan is happy as long as people are chasing after satisfying the flesh, and he is just as satisfied when they do something "spiritual" to satisfy a worldly desire.

Therefore, instead of spending energy trying to get people to sin, Satan invests into changing society's perception on life, and because people are more likely to believe what the majority of society believes, they quickly adopt the ideas he plants. These social infections are often so subtle that without the light of the

Word and the Spirit of God, they are almost impossible to detect.

SPIRIT OR BODY?

Out of the three parts that make up a human being, the spirit is the closest to God and is the point of connection with God. Anything from the spiritual realm is first perceived or captured by the spirit before being transmitted to the soul, and finally onto the body. Thus, the spirit is key to any form of human connection with God. Satan wants any spiritual awareness out of the way since the very belief in the existence of a spiritual reality is a potential hindrance to his plan.

The balance of power between the spirit and the body determines whether the soul is leaning toward salvation or toward condemnation. When the spirit has a greater influence over the entire being, the soul is leaning toward its salvation. However, when the body has a greater influence, the soul is leaning toward condemnation.

The spirit is the human connection to God. When the spirit is dominating, the soul moves toward its salvation. In other words, the soul is more exposed to divine influences that come through the spirit. Such a soul has no problem with godliness and submission to God. For this soul, life means fulfilling God's purpose. Therefore, it mainly lives for other people.

The body is the human connection to the physical world. When the body is dominating, the soul moves toward its condemnation. In other words, the soul is more exposed to worldly influences from the physical world that come through the body. Godliness is not appealing to this soul. It looks at life through the eyes of the body. For this soul, life means possessions, good health, pleasures, and ensuring the future. It lives mainly for self-preservation, and if it happens to do something good for someone else, then it is usually because self-gratification is the motive or there is the hope that someone will return the favor in the future.

To destroy humanity, Satan tries to put a conflict between the spirit and the body. In 1 Thessalonians 5:23, we read that there are only three parts to our being: spirit, soul, and body. According to God's design, human beings must strive to follow the leadership of the spirit, and Satan knows that all it takes to alter human nature for self-destruction is to plant a conflict between the spirit and body. The Apostle Paul speaks of the conflict in Galatians 5:16–17, saying, "I say then: Walk in the Spirit, and you shall not fulfill the lust of the flesh. For the flesh lusts against the Spirit, and the Spirit against the flesh; and these are contrary to one another, so that you do not do the things that you wish."

Although spirit, soul, and body are three distinct parts, there is no real way to isolate or influence them individually. Everything that affects one also affects the other parts, and they may or may not be affected in the same way.

Only two forces drive human life: the attraction to salvation (spiritual) and the attraction to condemnation (fleshly). This is because a human being is only exposed to two influences due to its nature of being made up of a spirit, soul, and body. The soul is *who* you are. The spirit is your vehicle in the spiritual realm and the body is your vehicle in the physical realm. The attraction to salvation is a force that wants to act on the spirit and the attraction to condemnation is the force that wants to act on the body.

In other words, human life is a series of choices the soul makes in deciding whether to follow the spirit or the body. We are constantly being attracted to either salvation or condemnation, eternal life or eternal separation from God. Even Jesus talks about the two choices in Matthew 7:13-14, saying, *"Enter by the narrow gate; for wide is the gate and broad is the way that leads to destruction, and there are many who go in by it. Because narrow is the gate and difficult is the way which leads to life, and there are few who find it."*

Jesus shows how the soul has only two choices: the broad way and the narrow way. The broad way is the way most souls take. It is comfortable for the body, even though it leads to eternal condemnation. On the contrary, even though the narrow way is difficult and only chosen by few souls, it leads to eternal life. All human beings, believing or unbelieving, knowingly or unknowingly, choose between these two ways.

GOD'S MODEL

God purposefully places the spirit above the soul and the body. In a harmonious working condition, the spirit captures the will of God from the spiritual realm, communicates that will to the soul, and the body executes the will on earth. This is how Adam functioned in his initial state.

Although the essence of a human being is his soul, the spirit is still superior to the soul and the body, because the divine piece of God every human being carries resides in the spirit. This is why Jesus says in John 6:63, *"It is the Spirit who gives life; the flesh profits nothing. The words that I speak to you are spirit, and they are life."* This means the spirit is the most important part of a human being. In fact, as long as the spirit influences the entire being, a soul lives in perfect alignment with God's purpose for its existence. In this model, humanity is predisposed for godliness and faith, because a strong divine influence from the spirit dominates the entire being.

SATAN'S MODEL

Satan aims to influence the soul by empowering the body. His model completely ignores the spirit, but seeks to empower the body in such a way that the body influences every decision the soul makes. Because these decisions are actually originating from the body, the model ultimately seeks for humanity to deny the existence of the soul and spirit. In this model, humanity is only aware of its natural existence.

That's why all nonbelievers ultimately deny the existence of the human spirit and soul. Because their soul's decisions are heavily influenced by the body, they have no connection to God whatsoever, and do not have any spiritual experience. They perceive their existence as being equal to any other animal found in nature with the only difference being the fact that they are smarter. Therefore, in the last phase of this model's evolution, before the second coming of Jesus Christ, the majority of the world denies the existence of the human spirit and the soul.

At this point in Satan's plan, humanity identifies self with only the body. It thinks there is no life after death and there is no accountability to a creator. Therefore, man is just another animal and should embrace his animal instincts instead of trying to control them as the Word of God commands us to do in Galatians 5:16, saying, *"Walk in the spirit and you shall not fulfill the lusts of the flesh."*

For such a person, everything in his life gravitates around survival, living for self-preservation only. That's why Satan's model promotes fairness above righteousness and where fairness becomes justice. Under this model, we must compromise to be able to live together, otherwise we are doomed to destroy one another.

This is a perfect recipe for ungodliness. God is not

fair, but He is just, and He does not compromise to coexist with darkness, but His very nature abolishes darkness utterly. For instance, the difference between lesbian, gay, bisexual, and transgender (LGBT) activism and civil rights activism in the tradition of Martin Luther King is found in the fact the LGBT activists ask for fairness, whereas civil rights activists asked for justice. Fairness is man's justice, but true justice is God's justice. This model ultimately promotes a spirit of compromise so that people bend morality to coexist with immorality and bend religious and cultural values to accommodate vices in the name of fairness—a type of survival.

When we place the body above the soul, Satan is able to gain full control of the soul. He makes his way slowly to the soul by making the entire being more aware of its physical senses than its spiritual existence. Being more aware of the physical reality makes us perceive self as essentially a body. Therefore, we are incapable of making connections with God since we can only make connections with God through the spirit.

Satan understands that his only gateway into a human being is the body. Therefore, he constantly entices the body to overpower the spirit. As we move forward in our story, we show how, in the end, Satan uses tactics and tools we are familiar with to condition people to live as if they were soulless and spiritless beings. He creates an illusion so that we would give in to sinful impulses while ignoring the subtle but deep desire to reconnect with God.

Satan already knows that mankind is a trinity. He is aware that his greatest obstacle is the connection Adam and Eve had with God, which is the spirit God breathed into them. Satan's goal, therefore, was to come up with a way to sever that connection between man and God. Even sin does not do this. As long as there is a spirit, a soul and a body in man, there is an open portal between God and man. Therefore, the only way to take the spirit out of the picture is to create an identity crisis—a total loss of spiritual awareness.

What will it take for humanity to lose its original spiritual awareness? How does Satan lead mankind to this state? These questions will be addressed in the next chapter.

CHAPTER 2

THE WORSHIP BATTLE

One way to disconnect mankind from God is to attack our innate desire to worship. Looking at the history of the Israelites and their walk with God, idolatry has always been the easiest and fastest path to calling down God's judgement upon themselves. In his efforts to leading the people of God to destruction, idolatry is by far Satan's most powerful and most successful weapon. From day one of our existence, mankind's natural predisposition to worship has become the devil's target. He exploits this feature of human nature in order to create a battleground in man's heart.

When human beings are not worshiping God, there is always something else they are worshiping. It is part of our divine nature to worship. Satan takes advantage of this particular aspect of human nature to turn humanity against God. All he needs to do is to find other things that can win man's heart. When something else takes God's place in man's heart, man becomes an idolater.

Merriam-Webster's online dictionary, defines worship as *"reverence offered to a divine being or supernatural power or an act of expressing such reverence."*[1] This definition fits the general understanding of worship as being an action.

However, Scripture takes worship one step further and introduces the notion of "true worship." Jesus explained that a true worshiper is the one who worships *"the Father in spirit and in truth"* (John 4:23).

It is not enough to offer reverence to God in order to be called a worshiper; the reverence must be offered in spirit and in truth. In addition, the greatest commandment states, *"You shall love the Lord your God with all your heart, with all your soul, and with all your mind"* (Matthew 22:36–40). Tying the greatest commandment to the definition of worship gives a glimpse into what God considers worship.

Human beings are always worshiping; when they are not worshiping the most high God, they are worshiping something else or someone else. When we worship God, we not only offer Him reverence, but we also place Him in a position that only He can occupy.

---

[1] Merriam-Webster, www.merriam-webster.com, (August 17th, 2016)

The moment He loses that unique position in the heart, soul, and mind, the worshiper falls into idolatry. How does God lose the unique position in man's heart, soul, and mind? Let's illustrate using the priority list.

THE PRIORITY LIST

The heart, mind, and soul can be compared to a priority list, and whatever occupies the highest position on that priority list is the object of worship. This makes it easy to fall into idolatry while still thinking we are worshiping God. A true disciple spends a lifetime trying to keep God at the top of the list. However, sometimes we fall to the impulses of the flesh, and for a short period of time, we worship other things.

People arrange their memories in the order of their importance. You are more likely to remember the things that are most important to you. In line with this concept, the human brain tends to do some form of routine check-up on the most important things to it. That's why you, once in a while, think about your wife, child, or an important e-mail you need to reply to. Because these things occupy an important position in your heart, soul, and mind, you are not only able to remember them, but also to keep them on the forefront of your mind.

In the same way, when God is the highest in your priority list, you will tend to think about Him a lot. Just as a husband or a wife would wonder if a particular decision or action would please or displease their spouse, you would also be constantly wondering whether God would be pleased or displeased with any of your actions or decisions. Therefore, whenever God occupies the first position in a person's priority list, God comes before everything or everyone else in this person's life. By that, I mean *everything or everyone*—wife, husband, girlfriend, boyfriend, children, career, job, and even self—would occupy a less important position on the list.

When God is at the top of the list, we will come into His presence with an attitude that puts Him first—regardless of what we are doing or where we are at. Examples of such an attitude would be:

- The work of God is more important than everything else.

- We tend to advance God's agenda rather than our own. For example, we would rather spend more time supporting missionary work than praying for a new car.

- Because we are inclined to try and please God, things such as forgiveness or humility become easier to practice. Forgiveness is no longer about whether one deserves it or not, but about whether God wants us to give it or not.

> Humility is no longer about avoiding clashes
> with another's ego, but about pleasing God.

When God is not first in the priority list, sin has an opportunity to sneak into our lives. It's just a matter of time before the person begins to commit sinful actions. Both the righteous life and the sinful life are defined by the order at the top of our priority list.

For most of mankind, "self" occupies the first position in the priority list. This is the state all animals live in, and that is why they put their survival above everything else. I personally think that the fall of Adam and Eve brought this condition upon animals. I don't think they were created selfish. Perhaps Paul agreed when he stated in Romans 8:20 that *"creation was subjected to futility, not willingly, but because of Him who subjected it in hope; because the creation itself also will be delivered from the bondage of corruption into the glorious liberty of the children of God."*

For a human being, when "self" occupies the first position in the list, he or she falls into idolatry. Remember, by design, human beings worship what occupies the first position in their priority list. That being said, sin is nothing other than idolatry. In the life of a believer, sin indicates that the order in their priority list has changed. Because pleasing God is no longer a top priority, what they expect from God becomes more important than what God expects from them.

Often, the kind of idolatry believers drift into is hard to detect. For example, when God is at the top of the list, we tend to put what He expects from us first, such as obeying His Word, spreading the Gospel, and supporting His work. However, when God is put down the priority list, even by one space, what the believer begins to expect from God become a bit more important, such as God meeting our needs, being merciful, or being gracious to us.

These two states are indicators between spiritual maturity and spiritual immaturity, spiritual strength and spiritual weakness. They can be used to measure how hot a believer's fire is. This doesn't mean that expecting God to be a provider makes us an idolater. It simply means that, when God is at the top of the list, we want to please Him more than we want Him to please us.

Believers who remove God from the top of the list tend to become sin-preaching intolerant. They behave like a cheating spouse would—always on the defensive when guilty and on the offensive to justify their actions. Because God may still be occupying a fairly high position on this believer's list, he or she may not realize that God is no longer at the top. At this point, he or she will even struggle to recognize and to eliminate things that have a negative impact on his or her relationship with God.

When Christ is the top priority, the believer instinctively eliminates anything or anyone that can affect his relationship with God. This is what Christ means when He says in Mark 9:47, *"If your eye causes you to sin, pluck it out. It is better for you to enter the kingdom of God with one eye, rather than having two eyes, to be cast into hell fire."* This believer doesn't even want to be tempted to put anything else at the top of the list.

The Bible tells us that the greatest commandment is to love God with all your heart, soul, and mind. Loving God with all your heart, soul, and mind is nothing other than placing Him at the top of your priority list. Therefore, the greatest commandment and the idea of true worship are the same thing. Remember, whatever occupies the first position in the priority list becomes the object of our worship. If this is not God, then it becomes idolatry. If loving God or worshiping Him is the greatest commandment, then it follows that idolatry is the greatest sin. That is why any sin is a form of idolatry.

Don't get me wrong. That which occupies the highest level of importance on our priority list is not to be confused with that which once in a while preoccupies the mind. For instance, being preoccupied with work does not mean work is more important than your children. In fact, caring for your children may be the driving force behind your temporary seriousness about work.

It is possible, however, for certain preoccupations

to escalate up the priority list until they become more important than they should be. For example, being preoccupied with work may cease to be part of a larger priority and become *the* priority to the point where your children are essentially forgotten. This leads to a change in mindset and ultimately to sin.

Worship is the blueprint of human nature. We are constantly prioritizing things based on how important they are. Besides those things which preoccupies man on a temporary basis, somewhere at the deepest point in our heart is the one thing we value the most. God is supposed to occupy that deep place in our hearts. Unfortunately, we often replace God with people or things of this world.

Every human being has a priority list. That means everyone worships, even atheists. But who is being worshiped? God or someone else—or *something* else? By choice or not, all people have something they love with all their heart, soul, and mind. Many simply don't realize that whatever they've placed at the top of their priority list does not belong there.

You may not be worshiping Satan, but he is still very satisfied when God is not at the top of your priority list. That's why Satan's main strategy is providing distractions. He doesn't like believers who have their eyes on God. That's why he spends a lot of time and energy trying to cut off the connection to God, which is our spirit. He knows that as long as you walk in the spirit, you have no weakness. He will brainwash people if that's what it takes to keep them from worshiping God, which in reality is what we hunger for and were created to do.

MAN'S SPIRIT IS THE HUMAN CONNECTION TO GOD'S REALM

The human spirit is the part of humanity that connects men to the realm in which God resides; therefore, the human spirit is in constant worship. No living being can be connected to God or know God and not have an attitude of worship. Our spirit knows more about God than the soul and the body do. God's splendor and greatness means that every creature with some kind of revelation of who He is will have an attitude of worship. That's why the human spirit is more likely to submit to God than the body is. That's also why, by just having a spirit, every human being on planet earth has a deep and sometimes buried desire for a relationship with the Creator.

The best way to think about this is to picture yourself face to face with a great personality such as a television superstar, a president, or a king. If you recognize the greatness of the person, the encounter will be more special than if it were with an ordinary person. In fact, you are more likely to be intimidated or feel inferior in their presence than if it were in the presence of an ordinary person. You may even give them special treatment because of who they are. In the same way, the human spirit is more likely to treat God differently because it is the part of the human being that is exposed to God.

The human spirit is a person's connection to God, the point of communication with God. The spirit is where a prophecy is deposited in the prophet, where a vision comes through to the seer, and where an inspiration from the Holy Spirit gets planted.

We can never receive anything from the spiritual world without it transitioning through the spirit. For example, on multiple occasions the Holy Spirit revealed to Jesus, through His Spirit, what people were thinking. Mark 2:8 says, *"Immediately, when Jesus perceived in his spirit* [spirit Man] *that they reasoned thus within themselves, He said to them, 'Why do you reason about these things in your hearts?'"* In addition, Romans 8:16 says that the Holy Spirit reveals things to our spirit: *"The Spirit* [spirit ghost] *Himself bears witness to our spirit* [spirit man] *that we are children of God."*

Satan wants to cut off any spiritual connection with God, and to do so, he doesn't want humanity to be aware of the spiritual realm. He wants humanity to perceive itself only as a physical body, as opposed to a spiritual creature. He knows that this deception infects humanity with an unconscious attitude of self-adoration or self-worship. The problem with self-adoration is that it is possible only when the body has more influence over the entire human being than the spirit.

When the body has a greater influence over the

entire being, Satan gains an advantage. When the spirit has more power than the body, the whole being is more sensitive to the things of God and can almost never fall into self-adoration. However, when the body has more power, the flesh exalts itself at the top of the priority list and the person falls into self-adoration.

Because the body also has the ability to control the entire being, Satan always sides with it. This is a perfect cover for deceiving a creature that was created to only worship God. As previously stated, it is impossible for a human being not to worship. If you are not worshiping God, then you are worshiping something else. When this happens, "self" rises at the top of the priority list and the body becomes the new god. Worshipping "self" makes this person an idolater and that makes Satan happy because idolaters are enemies of God.

Consequently, between the spirit, soul, and body, Satan's goal is to promote the body because, by default, the body will try to put itself at the top of the priority list. That's why Satan puts a lot of efforts into:

- Making Christians love the world more than they love the Kingdom of God.

- Vilifying preachers who emphasize the negative effect of sin on the believer's growth.

- Promoting preachers who turn Christians' eyes from spiritual growth to financial prosperity.

- Promoting "compromise" over "obedience" between parents and their children.
- Promoting wife-husband equality over the biblical model of husband leadership.
- Promoting sexual deviation over natural sex.
- Promoting sexual exploration over sexual purity and conservation.
- Promoting liberalism over foundational teachings.
- And promoting desecration over holiness.

The list above can get very long, but what we need to think about is how Satan promotes the body over the spirit in each of the above items. What you will find is that everything Satan promotes drives people into the opposing direction from which the Word of God would take them. Satan has a massive and sophisticated system that consists of fallen angels and enslaved human beings who work day and night to entice humanity into rebellion against God. This is done by trying to free the body from the control of the spirit—in more dramatic terms, by releasing the animal in us.

It's not easy for Satan to deceive humanity into worshiping self, because self is a very confusing and foreign concept to the man created in the image of God. God is selfless by nature. He is love, kindness, merciful, and more. All these characteristics of the nature of God are selfless. Because humanity has the nature of God, believe it or not, it also is a selfless creature, and all these characteristics of the divine nature (love, kindness, etc.) are the fabric of true human nature.

Humans are spirit in essence. That's why self is, or should be, a foreign concept to humanity, and a spirit will always tend to be selfless since it is mostly influenced by God. It is the portion of the divine nature in humans. Thus, it is difficult for the spirit of a human to exalt self or to become self-absorbed. In fact, the spirit doesn't even have a reason to do that since it doesn't compete for survival. The animal side, the body, is what can potentially become self-absorbed because it is constantly tempted to fight for survival.

When a human is self-absorbed, the spirit man is overpowered by the flesh. The body is just like an animal, and is selfish by nature. In more common terms, people call this "self-preservation." All animals in nature fight for self-perseveration ("self" is first). And people also fall into self-preservation when they start to look at things from the body's perspective, when they lose sight of the fact that they have a spirit that is connected to the Creator who put them on earth to fulfil His will.

Satan strives to redefine self as just a body. This is a deception where humanity identifies itself with its flesh only, the animal side, or the selfish side. The flesh is only a physical representation of who you are. The self-equals-body deception is the very meaning of Genesis 3:5, where the eyes of the spiritual, worshiper man, are no longer on God, but on self. ("You will be…self will be…because I will be…therefore, I eat the forbidden fruit…for once you see what you can have and feel," Satan says). Here man ceases to be the man who is spirit, soul, and flesh to become just flesh.

Satan applied the same technique when tempting the Lord Jesus in Matthew 4:1–11. He said to the Lord Jesus, *"If you are the son of God, command that these stones become bread."* Satan knew that Jesus Christ was well aware that He is both spirit and flesh. He also understood that tricking the Lord into defining Himself in terms of hungry flesh was not going to be easy. Therefore, he used the term *"Son of God"* in the hope that the selfless Lord, who is fasting for humanity's salvation, will act selfishly while thinking of Himself as the "Son of God." But the Lord maintained the revelation of who He was and said, *"Man shall not live by bread alone* [flesh/natural], *but by every word* [spiritual] *that proceeds from the mouth of God."*

The Lord maintained His definition of what the nature of humanity is and did not let the flesh alone dictate how to respond. Hence, having a strong spirit, He responded exactly the way His Father expected Him to. Jesus knew that He was not just flesh. He knew that three things put together define human nature: a spirit, a soul, and a body. Once again, the spirit is humanity's connection to the spiritual world, and the flesh is a connection to the natural world.

Depending on the soul's inclination, sometimes the natural world has a greater influence on us than the spiritual world does, and at other times, the spiritual world has a greater influence. When the spiritual world leads, God's nature is reflected, and when the natural world leads, the animal nature is reflected.

This choice of a soul to be inclined either toward the spirit or toward the flesh can predict whether the soul will be inclined toward good or toward evil. The divine nature stirs up selflessness and the animal nature stirs up selfishness. In the history of humanity, certain individuals were capable of manifesting a higher level of selflessness than others by tapping into the part of self that is divine, the spirit. Examples would be people such as Mother Teresa, Mahatma Gandhi, soldiers who display extraordinary courage by putting their lives in grave danger to save their companions in times of war, and individuals who sacrifice themselves or their families for some greater cause.

Satan's goal is to empower the body to the point where the spirit becomes almost nonexistent. It is in his interest that we define self as the body and therefore live to satisfy bodily lusts and desires (idolatry). Should Satan succeed, the world would begin to associate the meaning of life with desires and define fulfillment with how well we are able to satisfy those desires, rather than fulfilling the Creator's purpose. In the end, human desires define rules and the morality of society. As we move forward in our story, you will see how Satan deceives the majority of the world into the greatest sin of all, not only to provoke the God Most High, but also to unleash God's wrath upon humanity.

CHAPTER 3

THE FREEDOM CAMPAIGN

"Conformity is the jailer of freedom and the enemy of growth."
By John F. Kennedy

"Submit to God. Resist the Devil and he will flee from you."
— James 4:7

Corrupting humanity has never been an easy task for the Devil. He is desperate to see the greatest number of human souls in hell. Even though a seed of sin is already planted in humanity, Satan knows that the spirit inside man is always a problem because of its predisposition to seek God and His presence.

That is why the spirit in human beings is Satan's primary obstacle in the process of corrupting humanity. Satan wants to take the human spirit out of the picture, and to achieve that, he aims to throw all the composing parts of a human being into chaos. The composing parts include spirit, soul, and body.

> Human society can never follow Satan unless it is deceived.

Satan's goal is to plant a conflict between the spirit and the body. He uses "freedom" as a strategy to ultimately quiet the human spirit so that humanity becomes completely insensitive to the voice of God or to any spiritual influence from God. This is not true freedom, but a decoy freedom that deceives humanity, leads it away from God, and renders it blind to God's truth.

Who wouldn't want to be free? Satan began his "freedom" campaign in fifteenth-century Europe when he challenged old social structures. This was still a time of kings and subjects, masters and servants, or masters and slaves. Women had very limited or no rights. It was a rough time for most people. However, due to freedom ideas, it became a perfect time for a cultural revolution.

As ideas of freedom spread across Europe through

literature and art, those who embraced the ideas foresaw an opportunity to change, not only Europe, but humanity in a very positive way. Applications of these ideas were limitless, and in nations where they flourished, every aspect of human life was impacted very positively at first.

Unfortunately, Satan had a dark agenda for this movement. He ultimately wanted to use a deceptive "freedom" to set the stage for the antichrist government. He has three targets:

- Government
- Economics
- Family

THE GOVERNMENT AGENDA

Satan wants to change government systems around the world, because he is preparing for the ascension of the Antichrist as a world leader. Therefore, he needs a very stable and controllable system of government. He also needs this system to be distributed in all nations around the world. Ideas of freedom began to erode old views of government, then gradually, modern major democracies such as France and the United States began to take shape. This transformation was first felt in Europe and American; the rest of the World is just a matter of time.

The Antichrist's key message is "world salvation,"

which encompasses world peace, prosperity, and ensuring a better future. Satan wants a stable political system so that the Antichrist won't have to deal with civil wars and rebellions while he preaches world peace. Ronald Reagan once stated that *"Democracy is worth dying for, because it's the most deeply honorable form of government ever devised by man."* Just like president Reagan, many today believe that democracy is so far the best political system known to men. Democracy being a tool that could bring world peace and prosperity is a compelling argument to many. What may catch the world by surprise is the realization that democracy and God are mutually exclusive.

In addition, Satan wants the political system to be controllable. To control democracy, he needs to create the illusion that people have power. Meaning, he wants people to think that they have the power because of their ability to elect people into office that will pursue a particular agenda.

It's not easy to control a democratic system where there is rule of law. However, there is evidence that with enough money, even stable democracies such the United States can be controlled. Often, it is the financial backers of elected officials that really influence government policies.

Moreover, Satan wants this type of political system to be distributed throughout the world, meaning that he wants some level of uniformity of government across all nations in the world. A distributed political system opens the possibility for unification and renders management of such a large system easier. Democracy, as a human solution, is so far the best government system. Consequently, Satan won't need to exert much effort for the system to be adopted around the world. The only thing he desperately needs and doesn't have is time. It takes time for an entire nation to start thinking democratically and even more time for the entire globe to follow.

THE ECONOMIC AGENDA

When ideas of freedom are applied to economics, Satan sculpts an economic system that ultimately gives him control of the world's wealth: thus capitalism is born. For a human solution, capitalism is the best there is. So far, it has worked better than any other existing economic system. However, in the end, it sucks most of the wealth from the world economy and puts it into the hands of those Satan chooses for the task of ushering in the Antichrist.

When capitalism and democracy get combined, a system made of iron and clay is born. In the description of the vision of Nebuchadnezzar, Daniel says that the last universal empire on earth is represented by a mixture of iron and clay, a combination of strength and weakness. In his own words in chapter 2:41, Daniel states, *"The feet and toes, partly of potter's clay and partly of iron* [means that], *the kingdom shall be divided; yet the strength of the iron shall be in it, just as you saw the iron mixed with ceramic clay.*" A combination of capitalism and democracy reshapes the world into a relatively stable system of winners and losers with the super-rich on one hand and the super-poor on the other (iron and clay).

THE FAMILY AGENDA

Soon enough, these ideas of freedom start to challenge the traditional structure of the family. Again, at first, freedom thinkers and literature influence a lot of positive changes around the world. Satan must let the positive things happen first so that his agenda can sneak in behind them. In the beginning, it's about women's and children's protection against abuse. Then it is about equality between husbands and wives. Then slowly, things began to move into the territory of morality and faith. Satan wants to cut everyone loose so that he can remake them in his own image.

Parent-Children Power Struggle

While people enjoy a freer society than previously, Satan can now attempt to destroy the family using the same laws that were put in place to protect it. The fear of child abuse prosecution strips authority from parents who, by law, are bound to spoil their children. Soon enough, juvenile delinquency skyrockets. The correction children once enjoyed that helped them find an environment of unconditional love is now only given in government youth prisons—but without the love. And even in the realm of education, many are conditioned to trust the government more than parents for the education of children.

Child protection efforts have had unexpected results. At first, they save many lives, but later on, Satan pushed his agenda and conditioned society to unite in the search for abusers rather than uniting to better educate children. The tone is no longer "*it takes a whole village to raise a child.*" Because of paranoia, the people of the village neither trust each other to raise the child together nor do they have the time to do so. Now *it takes a whole village to turn a child rebellious against parents,* and the cost of child protection laws to society as a whole is much higher than not having the laws.

Husband-Wife Power Struggle

The same thing happened with laws that protect women. At first, they saved many lives, but then they changed the home atmosphere. It is no longer about protection against abuse. Instead, it's about who is greater than the other in the family home. Many wives take the "*who do you think you are?*" attitude while their husbands take a false "*you win*" attitude. Unfortunately, just like in the animal kingdom, men are naturally proud and territorial. They may try to accept a status quo for a while, but one day, their pride becomes even more important than family. As a result, many children are raised without fathers, and when the children ask, "Mom, why did dad leave us?" the answer is often: "He didn't say why."

It is similar to the Garden of Eden. Adam was too conservative and too hard to crack, but then when Eve was created, it turned out that she became a weakness of Adam, and therefore, an opportunity for Satan. However, just like the church and Christ, as long as Eve followed Adam, the couple walked according to what God instructed. Therefore, Satan continuously tried to isolate Eve so that whatever he whispered into her ears would then be repeated into Adam's ears.

Although unscriptural, the idea of equality between "husband and wife" in the home sounds logical and good for society. However, the cost is unimaginable to human society, not because the idea itself is bad, but because the powers of darkness have an agenda that require a power struggle between husband and wife in the family and home. Besides, in the divine model of marriage, Christ is above the church, and any attempt to change this order causes bad things to happen.

Catching up with Sodom and Gomorrah

A growing number of people believe so much in the decoy of freedom that the majority of the world is feeling the need for change. Soon enough, many believers and nonbelievers turn their back on the Word of God to make the law of the land their moral foundation. At first, they are raised from childhood to think that marriage is a contract between *two free and equal persons, a man and a woman*. At that point, it becomes only a contract between *two free and equal persons*, regardless of their genders.

In the end, marriage becomes irrelevant and the whole world is sailing for a pleasure trip. Sex is no longer regarded as a sacred act from which life can come, but it is vulgarized so that satisfying sexual needs no longer requires a special bond. Sex becomes a part of a set of activities that define pleasure. It has been placed in the same class with drinking, dining, or playing a sport. Humanity looks at this change as a normal psychological evolution, while in reality, it's just another stage in the evolution of sin.

Because it is difficult for Satan to acculturate individuals in a family setting, to control culture and education, he simply takes family out of the picture. When family barriers against vice fall, nothing else is strong enough to slow down the spread of rebellion against God. At this point, humanity is ready to welcome the Antichrist.

WHAT REALLY HAPPENS

What really happens is that humanity frees itself out from under God's dependency and becomes the crafter of its own destiny—its own meaning of life. This is the animal that sleeps in every human being, and Satan's scheme to awaken this man is to sell a "decoy freedom" to humanity so that, by pursuing freedom, humanity will unconsciously awaken the animal in itself.

This phenomenon is nothing other than rebellion of the flesh from under the control of the spirit. Satan convinces the world that a human being is 100 percent animal and nothing else. People are seduced by the idea that they can be authors of their own destinies, but once they accept it, an unprecedented transformation of human society begins—a transformation that Satan foresees as he introduces ideas of freedom into the world. He foresees it, not because he can see the future, but because this is his plan for humanity.

Ideas of freedom are spread around the world. Satan seeks to free the human body out from under the authority of the spirit and the soul. This is a deception that humanity embraces. It releases the human body from impulses of the human spirit to have a connection with God and puts humanity on a path of destruction.

As ideas of freedom progress through time and space, people will believe they have found the solution to all social problems. They believe principles of human freedom have the potential to stop repressive governments, bring economic prosperity, and emancipate every person living on the surface of the earth from alienating social systems. What humanity does not know is that Satan has orchestrated it all so that the greatest number of people will wind up in hell.

The message of freedom works for Satan, because

humanity is already very corrupt. When these ideas are first introduced, most human societies are brutal and repressive. The majority of people around the world are either enslaved or subjected to rulers who can treat them as they please. In other words, the world does not know freedom.

To fulfill his plan, Satan and his massive army of fallen angels have orchestrated three phases of implementation over thousands of years. The three phases represent three major steps Satan took in order to complete his agenda—a transformation of human society through a variety of society-conditioning tactics. What is accomplished during one period prepares the next until humanity turns away from God. Humanity thinks it is taking total control of its destiny, but in reality, it is just taking down divine safeguards against the powers of darkness and unconsciously surrendering to Satan.

DIVINE SAFEGUARDS

Divine safeguards are physical, spiritual, and psychological. They are conscious and unconscious security features God places within humanity to protect it against the spiritual world. Although humans are to live in a physical world, they are also spiritual beings and were created with the ability to operate in the spiritual world as well. Unfortunately, their connection to the spiritual world is Satan's target.

Spiritual Safeguards

Because of humanity's connection to both the spiritual and the physical world, mankind is susceptible to influences from both worlds. Therefore, God made sure that humans live in their home world, the physical world. However, He put in place barriers to limit the influence of the spiritual world into human lives. The barriers are in place to protect humanity from the spiritual world about which human beings know and understand very little. God's intent was not to completely disconnect humanity from the spiritual realm. On the contrary, Himself being spirit, He wants to have a relationship with human beings. The barriers are to keep humanity from being overwhelmed by spiritual powers of darkness. Therefore, to keep humanity safe, not only did He give human beings a measure of spiritual awareness by making them, in part, spiritual beings, but He also established laws or safeguard which govern interactions between the spiritual world and the natural world.

Spiritual Safeguards Examples

- Humans can allow or prevent any spiritual influences from entering into their lives (Ephesians 4:26:27, Revelation 3:20).

- Married women under the covering of their husbands are protected from certain harmful spiritual influences (1 Corinthians 11:9–10).

- Children who honor their parents have some amount of spiritual protection that result into a prolongation of their natural lives (Ephesians 6:2–3).
- God is always on the side of the innocent (Exodus 23:4).

Satan can never operate in the physical world if people don't allow him. In other words, any evil that Satan is able to initiate in the world can be associated with something specific people do to open the door for Satan's influence.

That describes spiritual safeguards, but what about the physical and psychological safeguards? The answer is that they are all connected. Because humans are primarily spiritual beings, almost every aspect of their natural lives is a projection or manifestation of their spiritual reality. For example, by sinning, the human spirit becomes sick and disturbs the balance of nature. His spiritual reality then translates into physical illnesses, diseases, and other physical pains. His loss of spiritual authority over nature translates into the rebellion of nature and the rebellion of nature into natural disasters and other problems related to his environment. I even believe that some wild animals are aggressive toward humans because of their spiritual state. We've simply lost the authority Adam had in the garden of Eden.

Physical Safeguards

Physical safeguards are limitations that God has imposed to limit what we can do physically, because such actions have negative spiritual repercussions. Take, for example, human sexuality. It is clearly unnatural for a man to have sexual intercourse with another man or a woman with another woman. These may seem like natural boundaries only, but they are also spiritual. Many people who come out of Satanism or demonic mysticism, such as the practice of magic (not illusionism), attest that an unnatural sexual act opens a door to dark spirits. Consequences of these acts often remain in families for generations. I elaborate more on this later in the book.

Examples of Physical Safeguards

- *Physiological composition* allows society to work with nature in creating identity. Examples would be things like the sexuality of men and women and racial differences.

For example, we influence gender identity based on physiological predispositions. Without these physiological markers, society fails to direct gender identity toward what nature intended, causing people to commit unnatural acts that open spiritual doors to powers that corrupt nature.

I believe that breaching these physiological boundaries can allow Satan to actually corrupt human physiology and things that did not exist in nature begin to appear. I believe this may be the case for many sexual deviations, such as pedophilia, bestiality, and homosexuality.

- *Geographic boundaries* make it harder for human societies to mix cultures. I elaborate on this later.

Any breach between the physical and the spiritual world affects a human being either positively or negatively. When a door is open for angels, something godly happens in the natural world, and when a door is open for Satan, eventually something ungodly happens.

Most blessings in people's lives are not random. They happen because someone opened a door for them to come through. They may also stop because someone closed the door. Out of ignorance, people may close the doors to their blessings and begin to experience misfortunes. Because they tend to look at such events as random, they attribute such misfortune as bad luck, not because they believe in luck, but just to say that it was random. In reality, they had closed a door of blessing so that the positive spiritual influences can no longer reach them.

Psychological Safeguards

Psychological safeguards are boundaries God puts in place to serve as an extra layer of security on top of spiritual and physical safeguards. Psychological boundaries develop as a result of identity and social differences. What is considered a value in one culture can be a vice in another culture.

Cultural difference is an example of a psychological barrier. Although there can be an exchange of values when multiple cultures mix, there can also be an exchange of vices. Thus, cultural difference is a psychological barrier in the sense that having different cultures makes people reluctant to copy vices from other cultures.

What men consider to be a value can be a vice in God's eyes and what men consider a vice may be a value in God's eyes. However, every culture in the world has things that God considers to be values and things that God considers to be vices. In fact, this is how a culture's morality should be measured. From God's perspective, some cultures are more corrupt than others.

It is understandable that God does not want the spread of vices. However, one question arises: does He also want the spread of values? Of course He does. The problem with mixing cultures is that it has the great potential of destroying psychological safeguards.

The more psychological safeguards fall, the more Satan's influence on society grows. When a culture mixes with another, the increase in values does not counteract the increase in vices. This is almost like washing white clothes with both bleach and motor oil. The clothes will be ruined and discarded as a result.

Let's suppose multiple cultures come together and they exchange values and vices. They are now one culture, richer in both values and vices. The increase in vices puts all those cultures closer to God's judgment, regardless of the increase in values. In other words, if we consider one of the original cultures, regardless of the increase in values in that culture, they now have more vices than before. From God's perspective, they are farther from Him, and therefore it becomes harder for them to reach salvation.

I believe this could be one of the reasons why God dispersed humans throughout the surface of the earth after they built the Tower of Babel in Genesis 11. The dispersal created new languages and cultures. Some theologians even believe that this is when God introduced the races.

The lower the moral degradation is, the higher the psychological safeguards are, and the less Satan can influence a culture. This equation is extremely important to God. Remember, God cares about the salvation of humanity, and He does not want us to go farther from salvation. For example, a culture that values virginity before marriage is more protected against satanic forces than one where people become sexually active before marriage. In this particular case, valuing virginity is the psychological safeguard. Similar psychological safeguards can be found in most cultures, whether the culture is Judeo-Christian or not.

Examples of Psychological Safeguards (*Some Social Values*)

- *Virginity before marriage*: This makes it more challenging for Satan to entice such a person into the sin of fornication and reduces options for adulterous individuals.

- *Belief that people pay for their good and evil deeds in their lifetime*: This makes it more challenging for Satan to entice such a person into stealing from or duping other people.

- *Belief in life after death*: This causes people to make better choices when they are still alive.

- *Belief in hierarchy* (all men are not equal): This makes it harder for Satan to corrupt many people at once. In a society where people believe in hierarchy, Satan would have to try to influence the one person at the top, and have him impose changes to the entire society. The rest of the people in that society may or may not choose to follow. However, the advantage this society has is the fact that God can still lead through one or few men as He has historically. I believe Satan doesn't like this type of society because it is highly unpredictable. One moment people could be worshipping idols, and the next, leadership changes and an entire nation starts to fast and repent of its sins before God (Jonah 3:5). This is also true for the opposite scenario. One moment people could be worshipping and serving God, and the next moment they are worshipping and serving an idol (Exodus 32:1). This society could move in the direction of deceit probably as easily as it can move in the direction of faith. For Satan, winning is highly volatile in this environment.

In contrast, an anti-hierarchy society is the ideal ecosystem for Satan's agenda. This is a society of rebels. By having an anti-authority attitude, it already is predisposed to be anti-God. At least not directly, but by opposing every authority, this society is more likely to oppose God Himself. Perhaps what Paul says to the Romans was meant for our times. He states that *"there is no authority except from God, and the authorities that exist are appointed by God. Therefore whoever resists the authority resists the ordinance of God, and those who resist will bring judgement on themselves"* (Romans 13:1-7). Later in this book, we see how our modern society, led by an antichrist spirit, not only benefits from nurturing rebellion, but also sets itself on a path that *"opposes and exalts* [itself] *above all that is called God"* (2 Thessalonian 2:4).

The notion of safeguards is key to understanding Satan's strategies. Thinking in terms of predisposition to believe or not to believe in the Gospel, safeguards may determine whether one is worth saving or not. In fact, the Bible contains stories of nations or people whose safeguards were so depleted that God was determined to exterminate them from the surface of the earth. Therefore, safeguards are Satan's primary target in human societies.

Satan knows that God loves the world, and over many millennia, Satan has come to the realization that corrupting people that are protected against corruption could be counterproductive. In addition, he has learned that taking down the safeguards is the best strategy for achieving humanity's annihilation. He used this strategy in Sodom and Gomorrah, and the two nations brought God's wrath upon themselves. Just as no parent enjoys spanking their children, God also does not enjoy punishing humanity. The only weapon Satan has against God is to turn humanity away from Him.

Humanity can reach a level where it can no longer be saved. Sodom and Gomorrah reached that level, Noah's generation reached that level, and many of the nations that were exterminated during the taking of Canaan by the Hebrews also reached that level. In these last days, Satan's primary focus is to turn not one person, not one nation, not even one continent, but the entire globe into the next Sodom and Gomorrah so that when the "*day of the Lord comes*" the only fate for the world is judgment.

Consequently, we are going to see a greater decrease in safeguards during the twenty-first century. Today, abortion is still a controversy, but perhaps tomorrow even those who claim to be Christians will make peace with it and find justification for its existence. Satan and his army of fallen angels are determined to take down the remaining safeguards faster than ever because they know that they have a short time.

To accomplish his goal, Satan uses an illusion of freedom to convince people that humanity is evolving, but what they don't realize is that their idea of freedom isn't what is causing humanity to evolve, but their hatred of godliness is what is creating the evolution.

It's not freedom they are embracing, but a spirit of antichrist as predicted in Scriptures. The new free-spirited, open-minded, irreligious citizen of the world is not a byproduct of the ideas of freedom as many would like to think, but this new type of earth tenant is a byproduct of a godless and rebellious spirit. All it produces is:

- Blasphemous language
- Blasphemous behaviors
- A media that hates God so much that no movie or television show finishes without mocking God or His people
- And many other immoral activities

For true believers, this will not be a surprise since Scripture has already warned us that these times would come in 2 Timothy 3:1–5 (emphasis added): *"But know this, that **in the last days** perilous times will come: For men will be lovers of themselves, lovers of money, boasters, proud, **blasphemers**, disobedient to parents, unthankful, unholy, unloving, unforgiving, slanderers, **without self-control**, brutal, **despisers of good**, traitors, headstrong, haughty, **lovers of pleasure rather than lovers of God."***

Now that you understand what Satan is looking to accomplish, you are ready to hear the story of how Satan conditions the world to become what it is today and what it becomes tomorrow.

UNIT 2

CONDITIONING IN THREE MAJOR PHASES

CHAPTER 4

AGE OF EXPRESSION
MAKE THEM BELIEVE THE ILLUSION

"The attitude of man toward the non-human environment has differed profoundly at different times. The Greeks, with their dread of hubris and their belief in a Necessity or Fate superior even to Zeus, carefully avoided what would have seemed to them insolence towards the universe. The Middle Ages carried submission much further: humility towards God was a Christian's first duty. Initiative was cramped by this attitude, and great originality was scarcely possible. The Renaissance restored human pride, but carried it to the point where it led to anarchy and disaster. Its works were largely undone by the Reformation and the Counter-reformation. But modern technique, while not

> *altogether favorable to the lordly individual of the Renaissance, has revived the sense of the collective power of human communities. Man, formerly too humble, begins to think of himself as almost a god."*
> – BERTRAND RUSSELL

> *And the Lord said, "My Spirit shall not strive with man forever, for he is indeed flesh."*
> – GENESIS 6:3

THE AGE OF Expression started when Adam and Eve fell into sin and continued until the establishment of the 1948 Universal Declaration of Human Rights (UDHR) order. The United Nations' UDHR marked the start of a campaign that exalted human natural life with a hidden satanic agenda. The goal was to deteriorate the belief that a human being is a trinity composed of spirit, soul, and body. Should the campaign be successful, the common belief becomes that a human being is only a body. This is the first milestone Satan wants to reach in his pursuit of the control of humanity.

> **Who you are and what you do physically is a shadow of your true self who is spirit.**

To understand what "Age of

Expression" means, let's first explain the concept of expression in our context. Given that human beings have a body and a spirit, they have the ability to operate in both the physical world and the spiritual world. The one thing that most of us do not understand is the fact that visible things originate from spiritual things. What we see physically is often the expression of what is in the spirit. Especially for human beings, the body is given to us so that we can express our spiritual reality with it, meaning that the body is the expression and the spirit is reality.

THE SHADOW OF REALITY

During the Age of Expression, the Devil used social engineering tactics to change our perception of human life. God created human beings so that the spirit is what triggers emotions inside the soul, and the physical body is a vehicle that expresses these emotions in the physical world. Remember, Satan is looking for an entry point or a way to influence the human soul. In the Age of Expression, he wants the body to replace the spirit as a source of instruction for the soul because it is easier for him to influence the body.

This is important to the Devil, because he ultimately wants people to believe that they only have natural lives and any claim about spirituality is superstition. As a result, people have no reason to submit their lives to God, because they believe that they only live once and nothing comes after death. Spending a lifetime being disciplined and holy becomes a waste of a life because living a holy life involves staying away from many natural pleasures.

Metaphorically, the body is a shadow of the inner spiritual being. In other words, it is a projection of the real self in the natural world. The body is just a form of illusion. Concepts such as freedom, love, joy, and happiness are spiritual in nature. During the Age of Expression, humanity is conditioned to believe that these emotions come from the body, meaning, the shadow becomes reality. A shadow's movement is not reality, but a reflection of reality. Feeling love in the body is normally a shadow of reality. The reality of love is a higher emotion that was generated by the inner spiritual self. Let's elaborate a bit more.

The Age of Expression is an age during which Satan's goal is to condition the world to believe that shadow is reality—the body becomes the reality and not the spirit within. The vehicle is in control and not the driver.

The body was intended to be a navigation vessel for the spirit and the soul. When the inner man, who is spirit, feels joy, the body mimics joy by producing chemicals which stimulate the body's senses for joy. When the inner man feels love, the body translates the love emotion into what physical senses interpret as love.

This original role of the body was essentially one of an interpreter. Most of the fundamental emotions of the body were supposed to be expressions of things much greater than what was expressed through physical senses. For instance, the feeling of true happiness can be expressed in our bodies. However, true happiness itself transcends all the cravings of our physical bodies. It cannot be obtained through natural things and, therefore, should not be defined as a particular physical emotion.

In the Age of Expression, Satan's goal is to deceive the man, who was created in the image of God, to become more aware of his physical reality instead of his spiritual reality. The end result is that most of what the body expresses won't be coming from the spirit. The human being becomes his physical reality, meaning that the spirit is no longer the only influence over the vessel. There is a power struggle between the spirit and the body.

You might feel compassion, which is in essence a divine and spiritual emotion, but the motive of your heart determines whether it is true compassion or not. Many people think they feel and show compassion, but a little introspection can reveal to them that their compassion was motivated by the hope of some sort of reward and not by compassion itself. In other words, their desire to show compassion came from a tendency to seek self-gratification. I call this *"it makes me feel good to help"* compassion.

In the same way, people often feel the shadow of love in their bodies. One way to test love to determine its source is to compare it with the spiritual love according to 1 Corinthians 13:4–7: *"Love suffers long and is kind; love does not envy; love does not parade itself, is not puffed up; does not behave rudely, does not seek its own, is not provoked, thinks no evil; does not rejoice in iniquity, but rejoices in the truth; bears all things, believes all things, hopes all things, endures all things."* If love fails this test, then what is being felt is some form of degraded representation of love.

This is why we have such a hard time loving our enemies, and yet Jesus set a clear difference between the false love and true love when He said in Matthew 5:43–44, *"You have heard that it was said, 'You shall love your neighbor and hate your enemy.' But I say to you, love your enemies, bless those who curse you, do good to those who hate you, and pray for those who spitefully use you and persecute you."* The reason why most people have a hard time with this type of love is because, during the Age of Expression, Satan successfully convinced them that they are only natural beings, meaning consciously or unconsciously they perceive themselves as much-evolved animals. Therefore, it is most natural for them to:

- Base their emotions on self-preservation and consequently love only those who love them
- To believe that enemies pose a real threat.

This is why I strongly believe that there is only one kind of love—*agape* love. All the other kinds of love, *eros*, and *phileo*, live in our bodies. In Greek, *agape* is God's love. *Eros* is the love between a man and a woman or in common terms romantic love. *Phileo* is brotherly love. *Agape* love transcends the natural body. In fact, whether it is love between a man and a woman or brotherly love, they are all different physical interpretations of *agape*. Their differences reside in what the soul chooses to make them.

When there is no *agape* love between a husband and wife, their *eros* love is doom to fail. For *eros* love to succeed, it must be an expression of *agape*. This is exactly what Christ felt for His church. Ephesians 5:25 says, *"Husbands, love your wives, just as Christ also loved the church and gave Himself for her."* Here Christ, the husband, expresses *agape* in the form of *eros* for his wife, the church. We tend to divorce because we do not strive to love our spouses with *agape* love.

Phileo love should be a true expression of *agape* love. This is the love that Jonathan felt for David. First Samuel 18:1 says, *"Now when he had finished speaking to Saul, the soul of Jonathan was knit to the soul of*

David, and Jonathan loved him as his own soul." This is also what Matthew 22:39 means by *"You shall love your neighbor as yourself."*

The Age of Expression is a period during which Satan and all his demons work to put a conflict between the spirit and the body so that humanity identifies self with the body. Consequently, the meaning of "self" shifts from being a "supernatural being living in a physical body" to a "super intelligent animal." Here Satan wants people to perceive the body as the only human reality.

Imagine the interaction between the spirit and the body being a song that goes as follows: *"Spirit feels, body expresses, spirit feels, body expresses."* These lyrics represent the expression of pure divine emotions such as *agape* love, happiness, or joy. Instead, the song sounds like: *"Body feels, body feels, body feels, body feels."* As a result, the man created in the image of God is living a lie. He seeks to feel love, happiness, and joy in the body. Unfortunately, the body can only express an illusion of these divine emotions and will never be able to generate them.

At this stage, the Devil's work is manifested when we see many of us pursuing the illusion of reality rather than actual reality, a complete mental dissociation of the spirit and the body. Originally, God wanted our reality to be the reality of the spirit, but with this deception, the body, which is a tool intended to be used to project our spiritual reality in the physical world, now becomes our reality.

For instance, an entire life can be wasted pursuing things that make the body feel happy, but the sentiments remain empty and nothing compared to what true happiness feels like. The same thing happens with love, joy, and all other spiritual things.

Considering love, for instance, many people live their entire lives without expressing *agape* love, not because they are incapable of it, but because the only reality they know is the reality of the body, which is an illusion of their true self. When people say, "I am happy," they are often not referring to true happiness, but a shadow of happiness that is produced by the body to facilitate our interactions in the physical world. They want it to mean happiness, but unfortunately it does not.

When a man finds a woman to love, often this love is confused with *agape* love, but in reality, it is just a physical attraction which might eventually fade away, and then he will feel like he no longer loves her and, consequently, ends up seeking a divorce.

Original State

    SPIRIT > REALITY

    BODY > PROJECTED REALITY

The Age of Expression
>   SPIRIT = THEORY
>   BODY > REALITY

As you can see in the second diagram, during the Age of Expression the spiritual reality is just an idea. Most people are not even sure they have a spirit. The body, on the other hand, is perceived as the human's new reality.

SATAN'S STRATEGY

Satan introduced ideas of "freedom" between the fourteenth and the seventeenth century, the period historians call the Renaissance (rebirth). The Renaissance was a cultural movement that set in motion fundamental transformations that the world's cultures are continuing to experience up to this day. The most outstanding phenomenon of the Renaissance was an unprecedented exchange of ideas due to the invention of the printing press. Satan presented very compelling ideas that have improve people's lives in many ways. However, the trade-off is costlier than anyone realizes.

INDIVIDUAL FREEDOM

Satan aimed to release man from any authority established by God. Therefore, his strategy is to promote the idea that man should be the only engineer of his destiny. It is the very spirit which later on leads to the "*falling away*" that Paul wrote about in 2 Thessalonians 2:3. People are introduced to the idea that no one should dictate what their lives should or should not be, that they are the authors of their own destinies. Consequently, ideas of "individual freedom" slowly began to alienate the human "natural safeguards" we discussed in chapter 3.

Before and during the Renaissance period, most people in Europe lived under repressive regimes of kings and emperors. "Individual freedom" was a strange notion, not only for Europeans, but also for the rest of the world. The Renaissance was a pivotal point, marking a time when humanity began to challenge all its old ways.

Now I will offend many!

Satan is the initiator of the Renaissance movement, and if he happens not to be, then he greatly took advantage of the movement. When everything was set into motion, he got to sit in the background, knowing that, in the end, he would get credit for all the "good" that came out the movement. He gets the credit because most of what came out of the Renaissance movement ultimately led to unbelief or what Paul calls the "*falling away*" in the end times.

For example, in the end, some people respond to the Bible in the following fashion: If "democracy" allowed homosexuality to become legal in society and God dislikes homosexuality, then homosexuality must come from Satan. However, if it comes from Satan, then Satan must be kind and tolerant. Not because they believe Satan is real, but because they are against the Word of God.

This reasoning doesn't necessarily mean that the person who thinks this way worships the Devil. To make a point, the person could be trying to say that the "power of the people" treats me better than God does. Or it could simply be that, for lack of faith in the Bible, the person is challenging biblical writings against homosexuality. Whatever their attitude may be, the ideas of individual freedom are what Satan uses to condition generation after generation into thinking that something is good as long as the vast majority agree that it is "good." The conditioning challenges the natural safeguards (see chapter 3 – Safeguards).

One of the natural safeguards is "*believing in hierarchy*" between the members of a society. There are natural hierarchies in both animal and human societies. These hierarchies are built naturally through spiritual, physical, and mental difference, which create interdependence. Differences are assets for a society, and interdependence defines how important the role of each member is. Depending on how important the role is, a member occupies a higher or lower position in the hierarchy.

Regardless of what people may think, the truth is that every individual in any given society plays a role that gives them either a higher status or a lower status in that society. Even in societies that function by the rule of law, we still see people with real power dominate so that the law—which is supposed to represent justice—becomes another tool in the hands of the privileged few. Does this mean that the natural order of things always prevails regardless of our efforts to make society fair and just?

Biblically, it doesn't matter how much we try to promote equality between husband and wife. Such an idea is against God's Word. In the end, equality between husband and wife hurts society more than it improves it. They are two naturally different beings who are created to play different roles.

The Bible compares marriage to the marriage of Christ and the church. If Christ is above the church, then this clearly defies what our generation perceives to be a good marriage. Through the "individual freedom" conditioning, Satan is able to progressively dissolve key natural safeguards that limited demonic activity in the human realm. As a result, violence, juvenile delinquency, and divorce become pandemic in families. People pursue the shadow of happiness and love, but they will never find actual happiness or love, because the body is now calling the shots.

SOCIAL FREEDOM

Satan also aims to break social boundaries that are basically leftovers of the original divine social and moral model. He plans to promote the idea that the voice of many people is more valuable than the voice of one man. This concept is commonly known as democracy. Some people like to quote a Latin proverb to explain this social phenomenon: *"Vox populi, vox Dei."* It means: *"The voice of the people is the voice of God."*

When we carefully examine this concept, we find that it is a clever deception. History proves to us that people of great wisdom and knowledge are always in a minority. Great ideas that changed the course of history and science did not emerge from populous masses.

On several occasions in history, one individual would rise above common beliefs and attempt to challenge what had been accepted as the truth. Sometimes such individuals were punished by death or exiled, and by the time everyone else caught up to what they were seeing, it was usually too late for that particular person. For example, in the sixteenth century, Galileo Galilei was persecuted by the Roman Catholic Church for saying that it is the earth that revolves around the sun and not the sun around the earth.

In this period, Satan wanted to promote a utopian idea of freedom, where the people, as a group in a society, craft the destiny of that society. Why is this idea a utopia?

DEMOCRACY IS AN ILLUSION OF FREEDOM

Freedom can only be obtained through Jesus Christ. Knowing Satan's agenda, two thousand years ago, Jesus told humanity in John 8:38 that *"if the Son makes you free, you shall be free indeed."* In other words, the world's freedom is not true freedom. Only the Son has the power to make you *"free indeed."*

True freedom Puts the Spirit above the Body

A free human being is a man whose spirit is in full control of his body and soul. Most world religions and spiritual movements teach this truth.

- **Hinduism**: Teaches nirvana, which means liberation.
- **Buddhism**: Teaches spiritual awakening. The name "Buddha" means "the awakened one."

So can we say that it is possible to reach true freedom through Buddhism, Hinduism, or any order spiritual movement that teaches this kind of freedom? The answer would be yes—if these paths were able to remove the guilt of sin. Consequently, even if you overcome passions of the body, which is extremely difficult to achieve, you will still need redemption from sin to escape God's judgment. Thus, the answer is no.

That is why Jesus Christ is the only way to true freedom. Why? Because *"without shedding of blood there is no remission of sin"* (Hebrews 9:22). Jesus reveals this mystery of the new blood deal between God and humanity in Matthew, saying, *"This is My blood of the new covenant, which is shed for many for the remission of sins"* (Matthew 26:28). Therefore, outside of Jesus Christ, any other path to freedom is a waste of good effort and time in pursuit of freedom. That's why Satan isn't worried about anyone pursuing these philosophies; he knows that he's got such a people exactly where he wants them to be.

In the end, Satan is just looking for people to go down with him. It doesn't make a difference to him if he cannot get you into clubs or make you kill someone as long as your sins are not forgiven. In fact, in these last days, Satan will promote teachings of Hinduism and Buddhism since they are very good at making people feel very spiritual.

RELIGIOUS FREEDOM

Religious freedom from the world's point of view is officially religious tolerance, and the unofficial message is that there are many paths to God, so you get to choose which one you like. This is a great achievement for humanity: the adoption of religious freedom laws in America and some European countries have stopped centuries of religious persecution. However, while all of this is happening, Satan relies on human nature and his army of fallen angels for the outcome he wants.

With the whole world exposed to multiple religions, Satan doesn't have a problem with any of them but one. He knows the way to God, the truth from God, and the life God wants to give to humanity. In previous centuries, he failed to eradicate the Gospel through the persecutions and false doctrines of the Roman Catholic Church.

Persecuting the primitive church resulted in a revival. Those who were persecuted in Jerusalem *"traveled as far as Phoenicia, Cyprus, and Antioch, preaching the word"* (Acts 11:19) and were able to spread the Gospel in regions surrounding Jerusalem. Many other nations got to hear the Gospel because of this strategy.

After Satan learned that true faith in Jesus Christ is not only immune to but also strengthen by persecution, he decided to opt for infiltration. In February of 313 AD, the Western Roman Emperor Constantine the First proclaimed the Edict of Milan, which officially stopped the persecution of Christians throughout the Roman Empire and marked the beginning of Catholicism. Catholicism introduced politics and several false doctrines including:

- Prayer to the saints
- The baptism of infants

- The worship of Mary, the mother of Jesus
- Beatification
- Purchase of entry into heaven with money (heavily practiced during the Crusades)

Infiltration ultimately failed because there was always a remnant that maintained the flame of the Holy Spirit. This remnant rose in the fifteenth century to bring reform. They had to be stopped, so Satan, in desperation, repeated his mistake and used persecution again. Persecution only strengthened the Reformers and the Protestant church was born. He is now sure that persecution doesn't work on true disciples of Christ. Therefore, he has rethought his strategy.

For his new strategy, he doesn't waste time trying to fight a Jesus who is already in people's hearts, but he wants to conquer the hearts before Jesus moves in. He was already working on the Renaissance project before the Reformation; the movement just got him sidetracked. He picked it up and continued to watch its incubation.

While Satan tried to contain the Reformation, on another front, his messengers pushed the freedom agenda in the Renaissance movement. At that point, no one saw the trade-offs as most people were deeply thinking and writing about all the different positive transformations freedom was bringing to society.

Finally, once the world was ready for his agenda on

religion, he laid it out in the Universal Declaration of Human Rights. Article 18 states, *"Everyone has the right to freedom of thought, conscience and religion; this right includes freedom to change his religion or belief, and freedom, either alone or in community with others and in public or private, to manifest his religion or belief in teaching, practice, worship and observance."* Bam! He said it straight—you are free to choose whatever religion you like. What a fantastic idea in a world ravaged by centuries of religious violence.

While we celebrate the idea that we can overcome our religious differences, Satan can almost smell the end of all religions. He is only interested in destroying Christianity. The other religions are collateral damage. The Universal Declaration of Human Rights has resonated throughout the entire globe, and freedom discussions multiplied and intensified. In America, it set the stage for questions such as:

- Should prayer be allowed in public institutions?

- Why should hospitals owned by religious organizations be exempt from providing contraceptives to women as a part of a medical insurance package?

- Why should the US president be sworn in on a Bible?

I am not saying that the path to God can only be achieved when all other religions are abolished. What I am saying is that humanity of the twenty-first century is being altered by powers of darkness such that we are losing an innate predisposition to search for God.

As twisted as I may sound, freedom of religion has enabled man-censured religion. It is a result of the sharing of ideas. People are exposed to several beliefs, so they develop an opinionated attitude toward faith. As a result, things that were once defined by religion for society are now being defined by people. Right and wrong is no longer a matter of the authority of the Word of God, but of people's opinions. Some people think one thing is right; other people think it is wrong. In the end, society rejects religions all together, and Satan congratulates the spirit of the antichrist for a job well done.

The new "free" man wants to free himself from God. Why? Because he's only a body, and his desires are opposed to the desires of the spirit, which is of the nature of God. The spirit aspires to return to God and to reconcile the soul with God so that it can be restored to its place in the presence of God.

The "free" man wants to kill the divine side of himself so that he can fully manifest the animal inside. The ideal "free" man is a man in full control of his life so that he has embraced most of his animal instincts, lives by them, and makes all the decisions of his life based on his reason and animal instincts.

Why does he want to free himself?

1. Because the spirit discourages the body from sinning: As the Bible says, *"Walk in the Spirit, and you shall not fulfill the lust of the flesh"* (Galatians 5:16). As long as this man is aware of the spirit, he is reminded of his divine nature and craves spiritual things.

2. Because the spirit reveals the filthiness of our sinful ways: The spirit or divine nature in us knows the holiness of God. Therefore, it is impossible for someone who walks by the spirit to purposely live a sinful life. He constantly sees the holiness of God, and therefore, he is at the same time able to perceive his corrupt nature and aspires to ascend into incorruptibility.

3. Because the spirit restrains his animal instincts: In 2 Corinthians 2:14, the Bible says, "But the natural man does not receive the things of the Spirit of God, for they are foolishness to him; nor can he know *them,* because they are spiritually discerned."

Our intellect finds believing in impalpable things foolish. It is wired to test everything. This is not necessarily a negative thing. Losing the ability to differentiate reality from the unreal is called insanity. However, the Creator made us with the ability to perceive things with our heart, or one could also say within our spirit. When one begins to perceive things with the spirit, reason gives room to faith, and consequently, the new direction (faith) becomes foolishness from the point of view of the flesh, because the new perspective is not in line with reason.

That's why Paul says that *"the things of the spirit are foolishness,* [not intelligible or rational] *to the animal man."* Paul goes further, saying, *"The animal man...cannot know the things of the spirit."* In other words, faith does not reside in the intellect but in the heart. Why? Because according to reason, it is insanity to see that which does not exist. What the spirit man perceives actually does exist, but it's just not perceptible by the animal man. The fact that something is not visible doesn't make it nonexistent. The fact that we can't prove the existence of aliens makes them neither existent nor nonexistent.

This is where humanity needs to realize that our belief system nowadays has been hijacked by scientific theories that originate from biased anti-religion scientists. Not being able to prove that God exists shouldn't mean that He either exists or doesn't exist. The outright pronouncement that God doesn't exist is the spirit of the Antichrist already at work.

Satan and his army have been working for thousands of years for a way to shut down our spiritual senses. They have been working since the fall of Adam and Eve in the Garden of Eden, ready to do anything to lead many to hell, even if it means infiltrating human society with incarnated demons (Genesis 6:4).

CHAPTER 5

AGE OF SENSES

MAKE THEM BELIEVE IT'S ALL ABOUT FEELINGS

THE NEXT STAGE in Satan's agenda is the Age of Senses. It began in 1948 at the Universal Declaration of Human Rights and will usher in the Age of Gods after the rapture of church. This is a period during which people are bombarded with information that appeals to their curiosity, intellect, emotions, feelings, and beliefs.

This new environment reshaped society so that all the shielding safeguards against the satanic realm collapse. In other words, doors to Satan's realm that were once closed have been opened and nothing stands in Satan's way for complete takeover.

Coming out of the Age of Expression, Satan has had

his greatest success with culture engineering. What he was not able to accomplish through mighty universal empires, he is able to achieve with a simple exchange of ideas through the Renaissance movement. He has learned that the most effective way to change society is simply to challenge that society with new ideas.

Now he focuses on using every tool at his disposal to intensify the exchange of information across cultures. His goal is to use technology to overwhelm old beliefs with new ones. To inject thoughts and suggest new ways, cultures, and morals. His ideas must become louder than cultures, belief systems, philosophies, traditions, and all other social voices.

During this era, Satan overcomes spiritual, physical, and psychological safeguards. This is no longer the era of primitive communication mediums, such as Egyptian papyrus used by the Greeks, but an era of advanced information technology. Satan has all the tools he needs to achieve deeper and faster social transformations. Therefore, his primary goal is maximum cultural symbiosis.

Because human beings are dynamic and prone to change, even closed societies ultimately change. They may evolve at a very slow pace, but they will eventually evolve, and the driving force behind the change determines the direction toward which these societies will evolve.

The American Civil Rights Movement in the

mid-twentieth century appealed to people's conscience to bring social change, but nowadays, many social change activists find the conscience of the people unreliable. The Civil Rights Movement lead by Martin Luther King Jr. relied on people's ability to choose between right and wrong to stop racial segregation. Nowadays those who are looking to bring about social change don't need to appeal to the conscience of the people. With enough money and control of the media, right can become wrong and wrong can become right. They don't need people to want the change. Technology and the media make the engineering of public opinion possible. Consequently, those who control the media have the power to slowly change our perceptions and even completely engineer the thinking of an entire new generation.

WHY AGE OF "SENSES"?

During the Age of Senses, people's feelings become the most important moral. Democracy has created a fairness environment for most of the world. Because people are free to think however they want and believe in whatever they like to believe in, many are open to conditioning.

They can be compared to children who are freed from parental control. With little knowledge and understanding of the universe they live in, they are left to do the bidding of whoever can provide more and better candy. However, they grow up to realize that they were duped and begin to wonder how their lives could have turned out had they stayed under their parents' guidance.

In the Age of Senses, Satan takes advantage of humanity's ignorance to turn it against God. Many are conditioned to chase pleasure because "feeling" is their only reality. Living now means pleasing oneself until self is satisfied. At this point, most people on the planet believe that a human being is just a body, and we only live one short life. Therefore, focusing on "self" intensifies during this age.

It is important for Satan to convince the world that they are just a "body," because only then will they will stop listening to their natural thirst for a relationship with God. Mass media and information technology dumps so much noise in people's lives that the voice of God fades away for the majority of people.

Many, at this point, believe that science and faith are contradictory, not because they read Scriptures and found actual contradictions, but because of hidden mocking messages found in movies, television shows, and all other media forms. They believe this fallacy, not because they've studied the Word of God and discovered contradictions with science, but because of speculations from others who are unfamiliar with the Bible like themselves.

Satan has given people many excuses as to why they

should not embrace salvation through Christ. Many say that they don't have a problem with Christ, but it's the preachers they don't trust. That is not such a terrible excuse; however, it is a hit for Satan. That's exactly why during this age he storms the world with preachers who are as mischievous as Satan himself. They preach, hoping that their message will yield a desire for the kingdom of heaven and thousands, probably millions of people follow them.

During the Age of Senses, people are too busy looking for pleasure that they become insensitive to the voice of God. The Word of God already predicted this, likening this age to Noah before the flood: They *"were eating and drinking, marrying and giving in marriage, until the day that Noah entered the ark."* (Matthew 24:38). This is why the rapture will be such a surprise for so many people.

CULTIVATION

Research in human communication shows that when people are immersed into the media for a long period of time, they begin to believe the social messages portrayed in the media. This area of research is called cultivation theory. Unfortunately, the new world picture that people who are exposed to cultivation acquire is often not an accurate picture of the world.

One of the most successful cultivation campaigns in history, with measurable results, is the one lead by lesbian, gay, bisexual, and transgender activists or the LGBT movement. There was a time when the media was hostile towards the LGBT people. However, looking at the past decade, public opinion changes about LGBT seem to correlate to the amount of LGBT content in the media. A recent exponential increase in LGBT content in television shows, movies, and other mass media tools appear to be helping with the shifting of public opinion in favor of the LGBTs, especial among young people in most western countries.

For centuries, whenever Satan wanted to destroy kingdoms and empires, sexuality has been his favorite ally. His formula is to corrupt an entire generation so that an entire culture becomes an abomination before God. Once the nation becomes saturated with sin, Satan won't have to do anything; God's judgment will subsequently follow. This is the reason why Sodom and Gomorrah were destroyed. It also is the reason why God wanted the Canaanites exterminated and their land given to the people of Israel.

Often, when a nation is infected with sexual immorality, there is no turning back. Sexual sins bring other sins or unclean living with them. Wherever you see sexual deviations, you will also find:

- Alcohol
- Drugs

- Unbelief
- Idolatry
- Incest
- Adultery
- And much more

In a society that undergoes a successful cultivation for sexual immorality, practices such as incest thrive. In other words, because people in that society are exposed to things such as sodomy, homosexuality, pedophilia, zoophilia (sex with animals), and other kinds of unnatural or deviant sexual behaviors, people in that society change their perspectives on sex. Pleasure becomes more important than the values society once held. Therefore, they develop a mindset of sexual exploration. Consequently, they slowly start to push any moral boundary pertaining to sexuality.

The Bible shows that this happened to the Roman society. Paul explains the Roman's sexual behavior saying that God *"gave them up to uncleanness, in the lusts of their hearts, to dishonor their bodies among themselves, who exchanged the truth of God for the lie, and worshiped and served the creature rather than the Creator, who is blessed forever… For this reason God gave them up to vile passions. For even their women exchanged the natural use for what is against nature. Likewise also the men, leaving the natural use of the woman, burned in their lust for one another, men with men committing what is shameful, and receiving in themselves the penalty of their error which was due"* (Romans 1:24–26).

Satan has had some success with this tactic. However, often in the past, too many natural safeguards hindered the disease's ability to spread. Human communities were still culturally very different and scattered all over the planet. For example, during the time of Sodom and Gomorrah, although many surrounding nations could have been infected by the sexual sins of Sodom and Gomorrah, it was still relatively difficult for the sexual culture of Sodom and Gomorrah to spread globally. Primitive communication and transportation means during that period limited Satan's agenda to just Sodom and Gomorrah and perhaps some surrounding nations.

In contrast, modern technology gives Satan untold acculturation power. One of his observable successes is the use of television to normalize homosexuality and other sexual deviations. His strategy is to bombard the world with media content that normalizes sexual behaviors that are against God's Word. Because he understands the science behind cultivation, he uses the media to engineer a new culture. Then the new culture yields a generation of people according to his own image. Not a tolerant generation, but a generation of people who are sexually curious.

For instance, since the early 1990s, there has been

an increase featuring of homosexuality in the media. Prominent movies actors are willing to play gay roles in movies and popular TV shows. For instance:

- 2010: Bradley Cooper in *Valentine's Day*
- 2009: Jim Carrey in *I Love You, Phillip Morris*
- 2007: Robert De Niro in *Stardust*
- 2006: Daniel Craig in *Infamous*
- 2005: Lena Headey in *Imagine Me And You*
- 2004: Emily Blunt in *My Summer Of Love*
- 2003: Jennifer Lopez in *Gigli*
- 2002: Julianne Moore in *The Hours*
- 2001: Naomi Watts in *Mulholland Drive*
- 1997: Greg Kinnear in *As Good As It Gets*
- 1993: Tom Hanks in *Philadelphia*
- 1993: Will Smith in *Six Degrees Of Separation*

This upward trend in LGBT activism has had notable effects on American society and presumably on the entire world. In the US, more and more states are legalizing gay marriage, and an increasing percentage of young people seem to be more open to the idea.

During the early stage of media technology development, LGBT activists already understood cultivation. They used their influence and money to bombard the world with content that portrayed what was once considered sexual immorality as the new norm. By overwhelming a hostile world with content of a different perspective, they were slowly able to shift public opinion in favor of the deviant sexuality. Some of the most popular and inspiring figures in cinema are featured as LGBT characters with roles that not only promote a good image, but also send a message with a profound impact on young people. In movies, these characters usually play roles such as:

- Best friend
- Kind friend
- Faithful friend
- Victim
- Wonderful adoptive parents
- Ignored but smart and outstanding corporate professional

It is just a matter of time before the majority in human society embraces sodomy and find themselves in rebellion against the Most High God. Sinful sexuality is one among many things Satan is using the media for acculturation.

Although some of us try to resist the media's influence, we all, consciously or unconsciously, are influenced by television, radio, newspapers, advertising, and the Internet. Believers and nonbelievers, rich and poor, and everyone in today's society are influenced by mass media one way or another on a daily basis:

- On one hand, it is helping philanthropists raise funds and communicate humanitarian messages, but on the other hand, it is stealing children's education from parents. Today, children get an increasing amount of their knowledge and life wisdom outside of the home.

- On one hand, it allows the Gospel to reach millions of people, but on the other hand, it is leading many to hell through pornography.

- On one hand, it raises awareness on war crimes, but on the other hand it is advertising jewelries made with "blood diamonds," which fund wars in regions of the world where diamonds come from.

- The list could go on and on.

Mass media is a true "good and evil" battleground, but the question remains: is it good or bad? Some may argue that it is good, some evil, and others both good and evil depending on how it is used. However, anything with the "good and evil" signature is to be watched carefully. This brings to mind the "good and evil" conversation between Eve and Satan in the Garden of Eden (Genesis 3:5). The Bible asks in James 3:11, *"Does a spring send forth fresh water and bitter from the same opening?"*

SATAN'S STRATEGY

During the Age of Senses, Satan's strategy can be broken down into three objectives:

1. The spread of an anti-Christian/anti-religion spirit around the world.
2. The use of new technology to engineer a new global society.
3. The storming of people's senses with a message that lures them into a world of lust and desire (senses).

As a result, humanity experiences the greatest cultural exchange ever, and Satan hijacks the exchange so that he can slip in his own ways. To motivate the exchange of information, he puts in place a greedy system that is based on principles of free market, meaning that the flow of information between cultures works in a free market fashion. Information becomes a product, and whoever can attract the most customers on the market wins.

Consequently, religions, philosophies, traditions and all social substances become tradable goods on the market, and while people are buying what they like on this market, Satan is also selling his products. People choose from one religion or from another, one philosophy or from another, and one tradition or from another, and what they are left with is only bits and pieces of each religion, philosophy, and tradition they were exposed to.

The fact that religion heavily relies on the integrity of its foundation means that many religions are at the brink of extinction. In other words, religion heavily depends on the follower's ability to abide by all its principles so that, when principles are followed only partially, the follower is no longer considered to be on the right path. Such a follower is no longer considered a true follower.

Just as consumer demand drives the value of goods in a free market, consumer demand also drives the value of religious and cultural ideologies. People choose what they like from multiple religions or cultures and reject the rest. Whatever they like becomes more valuable than other products on the market.

As a result, religion and traditions are no longer the foundation of society, but the volatile and evolving choices people make are. In other words, religion and traditions no longer determine what's right or wrong.

Instead, people are deciding what's right or wrong based on the ideological spectrum they are exposed to. It all becomes about how we feel about it.

This is where people redefine things. For instance, they say that:

- Jesus doesn't have to be the only Way, the only Truth, and the only Life.
- Marriage doesn't have to be between one man and one woman.
- The man doesn't have to be leader in a family as command by Scripture.
- Parents don't always know best for their children.
- The word "child" doesn't have to mean offspring; it can also mean "adopted."
- The word "father" or "mother" doesn't have to mean "the one who produced a child." It can also mean "the one who is playing the role of a father or a mother."
- Having male organs doesn't have to mean you are a boy or a man.
- Having female organs doesn't have to mean you are a girl or a woman.

In the Age of Senses, Satan makes extraordinary progress in conditioning the world; however, what he plants is still just a seed that must grow and be ready for the harvest. The next chapter talks about the harvest. What happens in the end? What is the final condition of humanity?

CHAPTER 6

AGE OF THE GODS
MAKE THEM BELIEVE THEY ARE GODS

The Age of the Gods is born out of thousands of years of social conditioning. This is payday for Satan and his army of demons. In this age, Satan has finished making the necessary social changes and is waiting for the right opportunity to officially govern the world for the short amount of time he has left. Two things are important during this age: first, the human global living-conditions and, second, the global spiritual and philosophical mindset.

The Age of the Gods is harvest time for Satan. He's worked for thousands of years planting seeds in humanity. To condition societies, he's used:

- Demonic worship, such as ancient religions and worships.
- Universal empires (Babylonian, Persian, Greek, and Roman, Ottoman, American and whatever comes next).
- Universal religious entities with extraordinary political power (Roman Catholicism, Islam under the Ottoman Empire).
- Mass media to engineer social values through what communication researchers call "agenda setting, hegemony, and cultivation."

AFTER THE FALL

After the fall of Adam and Eve, humanity was still very connected to God. Human beings were living nostalgically of what life had been like in the Garden of Eden. Although they did not know what life was like in the Garden of Eden, they hadn't completely lost their spiritual instincts.

They still had a strong urge to live in the presence of God and their spiritual senses were still strong. Cain and Abel, both born after the Fall, still heard the voice of God. In fact, they wanted Him so badly that Cain killed his brother out of jealousy for his brother's superior relationship with God. Even after killing his brother, he still heard the voice of God and was very well aware of the control God had over his life. Thus he bargained with God for his punishment saying, *"My punishment is greater than I can bear! 14 Surely You have driven me out this day from the face of the ground; I shall be hidden from Your face; I shall be a fugitive and a vagabond on the earth, and it will happen that anyone who finds me will kill me"* (Genesis 4:13–41).

Clearly, this first human society had an understanding of who God was. Although they were already experiencing the consequences of sin, they still cherished a relationship with their Maker. Sin has disrupted the creation balance and introduced the struggle for survival. Therefore, many are drifting away from God due to life conditions outside of Eden.

HOW WE GOT HERE

This primitive human society that developed shortly after the Fall was vulnerable. Sin continued to expand the distance between humanity and God. Food became hard to find, and life was a struggle. Everyone was trying to survive. Satan wanted to take advantage of this situation, but it was a big challenge because most people still know who God was and they feared Him. Therefore, Satan began to take small steps to fulfil his plan.

Satan knew that the plan for humanity's salvation was already in motion, so his goal consisted, not only in further corrupting the entire creation of God, but also in leading as many souls as possible into condemnation. How did he know about the plan of salvation? At that point, the plan was not a secret. God had already revealed that humanity would be saved. In fact, it will not only be saved, but it became a problem for Satan. God gave Satan a hint of His salvation plan in Genesis 3:15, when he said:

> *"And I will put enmity*
> *Between you and the woman,*
> *And between your seed and her Seed;*
> *He shall bruise your head,*
> *And you shall bruise His heel."*

Satan took his time in making small steps toward humanity's total corruption. Every step took humanity farther from God. It intensified sin and increased immorality in the world through the sharing of vices and values. The increase in values had absolutely no meaning to God due to the increase in vices.

STEP 1: DEMONIC WORSHIP

First, Satan decided to erase the nostalgia of Eden from the fabric of the first human society through demonic worship. He seduced the world into idolatry, but mainly through the worship of demons. Soon, many people no longer possessed the knowledge of how to worship the Most High God. Therefore, they were lured into worshiping creations of God (stars, mountains, forces of nature). It was such an easy game for Satan to play since that society was desperate for survival. Sometimes, when superstition became too successful, he even got people to worship some of his demons as gods.

These demons are commonly known as mythological gods in ancient history. You find them in the history of most societies around the world, such as Zeus and Athena of the Greeks and Osiris and Isis of Egypt.

Demonic worship successfully redirected human longing for the presence of God and transferred it to the wrong god. In search for safety and a better life, that young society began to compensate desire for God with demonic worship. Slowly but surely, over a long period of time, the knowledge about God that had been passed down from generation to generation got erased. The belief in many gods became the norm, and our primitive ancestors could no longer hear the voice of God as clearly as Cain or Abel once had.

Demonic worship went on for many centuries. However, the human desire for worship still bothered Satan. He knew that at any moment, if the Most High God called, man would abandon their false gods and run back to Him. Nevertheless, Satan considered this particular social transformation a step toward a greater transformation, which will have a greater impact on the human ability to recognize and obey the voice of their Creator.

STEP 2: UNIVERSAL EMPIRES

To take the primitive society further down the wrong path, Satan took things even further. He knew that worshiping other gods did not guarantee that humanity wouldn't go running back to God whenever He called. Therefore, he wanted to increase sin in human society. To do so, he tried to force social change by making man impose new ways of life onto another man. During that period, Satan's strategy was to create global kingdoms so that every kingdom would be introduced to even greater abominations than they had known. Universal kingdoms was the framework of Satan's entire plan.

In other words, Satan used universal empires as a way to efficiently lure the greatest number of people around the world onto his side. In fact, on several occasions, God revealed this truth to Daniel: First, in Daniel chapter 2 through the vision of Babylonian emperor Nebuchadnezzar and, second, to Daniel himself through the *"vision of the four beasts"* in Daniel chapter 7. In both visions, God warned His children about universal empires.

Long before the revelations in the book of Daniel, Satan had already attempted to establish a universal empire in the world. Genesis 10:9–10 and Genesis 11:1–7 talk about the first world empire built by Nimrod at Babel—Satan's very first social engineering attempt. According to Scripture, the dissolution of this empire is the very reason why God introduced languages into the world to make such attempts difficult in the future. Even in Daniel's visions, God did not allow humanity to be completely lost. All of these empires reached a tipping point where God decided to end them.

STEP 3: UNIVERSAL RELIGIONS WITH EXTRAORDINARY POLITICAL POWER

The Roman Empire, encountered a powerful enemy, one that was supposed to *"bruise [Satan's] head" (Genesis 3:15)*. During the first and second century AD, the Gospel was spreading fast and was starting to transform the cultural and spiritual landscape wherever it touched throughout the Roman Empire. It practically created a new spiritual battlefront for Satan. Until the coming of the Gospel during the first half of the first century AD, Israel was the only real spiritual battleground for Satan. Other nations were still worshiping idols and did not know who the most high God was. Therefore, the spreading of the Gospel became a new threat that an instrument of acculturation such as a universal empire could not handle.

Before the arrival of the Gospel, the only challenge to the transformation brought by universal empires were of society's natural safeguards. Satan only needed time to be able to take down the natural safeguards. That's why, historically, Satan has spent more time trying to find effective ways to bring social change than he has spent working on change itself. It often took many years of wars, conquests, and bloodshed to build great cultural shapers such as the Babylonian, the Persian, the Macedonian, and the Roman Empires. But once a universal empire was established, cultural change was almost unavoidable. Because most of the world did not know about God, people's spiritual beliefs were not much of a challenge for Satan. The Gospel not only came to introduce nations to God, but it also had the potential to undo the increase in vices that universal empires brought.

Therefore, Satan had to adapt universal empires to the new challenge. He wanted not only to allow cultural exchange, but also wanted to transform belief systems to counter the Gospel. As discussed in chapter 3, Satan promotes cultural exchange, mainly because it increases vices and not so much for its ability to increase values in a society. Therefore, after the Gospel is introduced into the world, Satan had to also worry about the effect nations that have been touched by the Gospel would have on nations within universal empires such as Rome or the Ottoman empire. But as Paul stated, *"It is the power of God to Salvation for everyone who believes" (Roman 1:16).* Because of that, Satan also began to use universal religions to deprogram society of the truth. During Rome, Satan realized that salvation was given to humanity through Jesus Christ. After the persecution of those carrying the message of salvation to the world failed, Satan decided to use the universal empire technique with a new religion twist to stop the Gospel from spreading.

He realized that he could not stop the Gospel. Therefore, he began to impose false religions around the world. The Roman Catholic Church and Islam went out into the world to conquer and convert. In some cases, it was convert or die. At different periods of history, those two religions were so powerful politically that they practically created new societies, cultures, and civilizations. They were not just universal empires or religions, but hybrids of both.

With universal religions, Satan killed two birds with one stone. He not only got the result a universal empire would produce, but he also was able to indoctrinate the whole world with false salvation doctrines. As a result, millions began to seek a decoy God that resulted in the practice of abominations and being lead far from the real God.

STEP 4: MASS MEDIA

The first three steps worked, but only to a limited extent due to the many natural safeguards that were still in place (see chapter 3). Although universal empires and religions have left many nations and cultures with several things in common, there are still significant social and psychological differences among them.

The last instrument Satan used to take down the

natural safeguards of humanity was mass media. The invention of mass media enabled him to spread his thinking much faster. In one century, Satan was able to do what universal empires and religions could not accomplish in five thousand years.

BECOMING GODS

The Age of Senses was the harvest time for both the Kingdom of God and the kingdom of darkness. Jesus talked about this harvest in Matthew 13:29, saying, *"Lest while you gather up the tares you also uproot the wheat with them. Let both grow together until the harvest."* This meant that God knows what Satan has been doing. But because there are still souls that thirst for Him, He'd rather let the entire creation suffer corruption than lose those souls.

The Age of Senses is harvest time for Satan and his army of demons. He's been planting for centuries, and what he planted is now ripe and ready to be collected. In other words, the Devil has been trying to condition the world so that people would perceive themselves only as physical beings as opposed to spiritual beings living in a physical body. Satan's ability to operate among man is extraordinarily high because he has almost full control over their bodies. All he needs to do is control their pleasure availability and they will go in whatever direction he takes them.

In the Age of the Gods, Satan has finished making

the necessary social changes, and only awaits the right opportunity to officially govern the world for the short amount of time he has left.

LIVING CONDITIONS

During this age, living conditions on earth have not improved. On the contrary, they have become worse. Scientific advancements have the potential to eradicate famine and many diseases. However, free market makes this impossible. While those who own patents on groundbreaking scientific discoveries enjoy profits, millions continue to suffer famine and disease due to lack of money. The rich are getting richer than ever and the poor are poorer than ever.

You may be wondering how I arrived at these conclusions. Luke 21:11 talks about the world's living conditions before the end. He writes that *"there will be...famines and pestilences; and there will be fearful sights and great signs from heaven."* The Bible clearly indicates that, science or no science, famine and disease will not go away.

Although living conditions are still not good, the world, however, reaches a point where it becomes hopeful. During the Age of the Gods, people think they are the crafters of their own destinies. They no longer believe in God. In fact, they blame religions for the lack of peace in the world. Humanity relies on its own potential. Therefore, it says, *"Peace and safety!*" as Paul predicts in 1 Thessalonians 5:3. What humanity doesn't realize is the fact that a lot of time and effort has been invested, for thousands of years, into the engineering of its new mindset.

SPIRITUAL AND PHILOSOPHICAL MINDSET

During the Age of the Gods, the majority of the world does not believe in any form of spirituality. They do not believe in spirituality, because in coming out of the Age of Senses, they have been conditioned to see themselves as biological organisms. They believe a human being is only a body and has no soul or spirit. Therefore, there is no life after death or any other dimension that people can live in other than the natural world.

The small minority that still believe in the spiritual world is divided into many different factions. These are the remnants who represent what's left of religion from the Age of Senses. Whatever is left is so insignificant that it doesn't look anything like the old religions, despite what these small groups may claim. However, what's left of religion is a diluted, mixed, and tweaked version of the original due to a lot of compromise introduced during the previous age.

The Age of Senses was the age when the gods started to awaken. This is a generation of people who were conditioned from birth to question beliefs, traditions, and even nature itself. Although conditioned, many who believed in the spiritual realm saw the necessity of compromise, because they believed that they were improving their beliefs. For example, this is when the church legalized sodomy, abortion, and many other things that did not exist in the primitive church. Though perhaps not as grave, I am sure such compromises exist in most other major religions. Christianity is just a primary target.

Philosophically, the world has its mind set to enjoying everyday life. Imagine a world that's not preparing for the end of the world, a world in which the only god around is the individual and the only enemy around is anything that threatens social stability. Most people have one goal in life: amassing wealth to enjoy life.

It is a world where believing in the Bible is insanity, because the majority of the world considers the Bible an enemy of world peace. The antichrist spirit has convinced even the least knowledgeable in theology that there can never be peace in the world as long as people are still following religious principles. At this point, the nation of Israel is either close to being attacked or Satan is still compressing tension against it.

UNIT 3

WHAT HAPPENS IN THE END?

CHAPTER 7

CLUELESS

HOW TO RECEIVE JESUS AND END UP IN HELL

One of the greatest challenges Satan faces during the execution of his plan is the church. Let's be clear. The church is not a particular denomination, but the body of born-again believers around the world. Thus, everything Satan does during the three stages of his plan is ultimately aimed at the church. The presence of a strong church on earth has the potential of making things very difficult for him. Therefore, he crafted the entire plan so that, in the end, many Christians are conditioned toward an unbiblical mindset of their position with God. As a result, many Christians:

- Become insensitive to the voice of the Holy Spirit in regard to sin.

- No longer submit to the Word of God, but are very opinionated in regards to it.

- Still believe that they are spiritual beings while loving pleasure very much and are not looking forward to heaven.

- Only respond to preaching that stimulates their senses.

- Have also become the gods of their own lives. Compared to nonbelievers, the only difference is the fact they've convinced themselves that they are saved.

THE "THORNS EFFECT": SPIRITUAL RETARDATION

In this age, conditioning has the "thorns effect" as described in Matthew 13:22. Jesus talks about a heart that cares so much about the natural life and worldly possessions that the seed of the Gospel becomes unfruitful. In his own words, Jesus states that *"the cares of this world and the deceitfulness of riches choke the word, and he becomes unfruitful."* People are conditioned to attach so much value to their natural life that the things of God matter less, and to some, they do not matter at all.

During the Age of Expression, the church went

through many different phases. However, it thrived and did an incredible missionary work. Almost every nation on the planet has heard the Gospel, and many believers around the world continue to spread the Good News of salvation.

During the Age of Senses, the church began to experience problems. Satan was finally in possession of more advanced information technology to maximize societal conditioning. Once people started believing that they are only bodies and not spirits living in bodies, the Gospel found very few hearts where it could grow.

By the time the Age of the Gods started, Christians believed that they were following Christ, but in reality, *"the cares of this world and the deceitfulness of riches"* has rendered them incapable of trusting in God. They have been conditioned to only relate to things that appealed to their senses. They see themselves primarily as bodies. The only reality they respond to is the physical world. As a result, the Good News is no longer about the forgiveness of sin through Jesus Christ, but how to enjoy everyday life on earth. Conditioning has affected even the message of the Gospel so that it becomes about caring for the natural man instead of salvation of the soul.

When conditioning reached its targeted level, beside the remnants, the majority of Christians around the world become spiritually retarded. The only thing Christian about them is the fact that they *claim* to be

Christians. Spiritually, they are forty years old with the mind of one-year-olds.

- They clothe themselves like the world.
- They speak like the world.
- They copy everything the world does.
- Abortion is normal if one wants happiness on earth.
- Divorce is normal if one wants happiness on earth.
- The Bible calls us saints, but many, incapable of walking in the Spirit, embrace the idea that we are sinners.
- Homosexuality is widely accepted.
- etc.

UNABLE TO SUBMIT TO ANYONE AND GOD

God's leadership is not a majority leadership. Scripture and nature show that God always leads through one individual. Perhaps the animal world isn't as corrupt as humans because the animal world still uses this model. Several times in history, the majority has caught up to a small enlightened minority after a long period during which the minority was persecuted because of its views and ideas.

In a world that is already off the path it was created to take, the one individual or minority leader model does not work. For instance, a nation should normally have one leader established by God at the top. Looking at such biblical figures, this leader is primarily a servant of God. He is at the top to fulfil God's will in his nation. Unfortunately, in a society where sin has already separated people from God, there is no way to ensure that the one at the top is God's chosen.

This is the reason why, throughout its history, the nation of Israel has struggled so much to implement a theocracy on earth. Every tiny rebellion against God meant separation from the presence of God. Consequently, the system collapsed. Sin brought imposters or rulers that God did not establish. Because imposter kings and queens are not led by the Spirit of God, by default, they lead the entire nation away from God.

In the final humanity state, people view leadership as a function, and not as a societal ranking factor. This comes from the idea that *"all men are equal,"* which is biblically not true. Satan wants people to become incapable of submitting to anyone in the end. That is why he conditions society to reject any form of innate authority, replacing it with institutional authority.

Although it seems that God asks people to submit to other people, in reality, what He asks is for people to submit to Him. When you submit to an authority established by God, you are not submitting to that authority, but to God Himself. Therefore, not submitting is rebellion against God.

In some sense, this is also true in society. In most democratic institutions, for instance, being in a position of leadership is supposed to be just a position, meaning that the leader's authority comes from the position he or she occupies. Outside of the scope of this authority, the individual is considered equal to everyone else. Where does your boss's authority come from? He is not born with it, but the company gave him the authority. Outside of work, he is arguably your "equal."

One key difference between the authority that social institutions give and divine authority is how both society and God find their human assets. When a social institution is looking for a human asset, it looks for skills or talents. Sometimes social institutions find the right person and sometimes they don't. That's the reason why people get fired from jobs. On the other hand, when God is looking to establish someone in a particular function, He creates the person. Therefore, He puts in him all the required skills and talents. God's human asset is a perfect and irreplaceable asset. That's why, within the scope of the position, he can exercise full divine authority.

DOUBLE AGENT SATAN

Satan plays the role of a double agent to lure humanity into full rebellion against God's established authorities. To fully understand how he plays the role of a double agent, we first need to realize that Satan is operating in a broken world where most of God's established authorities are separated from God because of sin. Although they are separated from God, they still have the skills and talents God placed in them when He created them. Because of that, even without God's influence in their lives, they do not completely deviate from what they were created to do, even when Satan deceives them. This is another aspect of the "natural safeguards" (see chapter 3) that all human beings have. How then does Satan become a double agent?

Satan doesn't like the fact that people believe in the innate divine authority in kings, parents, husbands and other forms of societal authorities. Therefore, he floods the world with people who abuse others. Satan is able to do this because the world is already corrupt with sin, and he takes advantage of the fact that the authorities are disconnected from God and are often far from where God intended them to be. Consequently, some bad kings torture, starve, kill, and abuse their people. Among loving parents and husbands are also those who physically and verbally abuse their children and wives. Satan's aim is for the world to question and then reject these authorities.

While Satan brings suffering in the lives of millions of people through established authority, at the same time, he slowly suggests that people free themselves from the authority. Here he is a double agent who is working for both "good" and evil. He plays the role of the evil authority so that people will rebel against the authority itself, and then he also plays the role of the social thinker who suggests an alternative to these authorities. Consequently, people reject divine institutions to embrace human institutions. What they don't realize is that human institutions are just the best painkiller for an advanced cancer called sin. Let me explain.

Many would agree that democracy is, so far, the best governing system humans have ever come up with. It allows people to define their own futures and the future of a society. In addition, history indicates that in democratic societies wealth distribution is fairer than in other form of government. Clearly, democracy may be looked at as one of the greatest inventions of the past two or three centuries. Unfortunately, it is nothing but another Satanist plot against divine institutions. Christians who live on earth during the reign of the Antichrist are able to see what democracy turns society into.

Satan understands that it is difficult to initiate a massive rebellion against God in a society where most people have strong ties with religion. Many get offended when their religious beliefs are criticized. Even those who do not consider themselves religious may still identify as belonging to a particular religion due to how or where they were raised. Therefore, Satan knows that a massive attack against the legitimacy of certain religions can backfire.

So he takes his time and introduces "ideas of freedom" as a first step to humanity's rebellion against God. These ideas are the seeds that grow as they are fed by propaganda against fundamental structures that protect human society against total spiritual collapse. The structures include government, family, and society in general. As these ideas spread, Satan places legions of demons on multiple fronts. Their targets are world government, the control of world wealth, and the destruction of family and social values.

WORLD GOVERNMENT

On the government front, Satan sends his soldiers to propagate the idea that "the voice of the people is the voice of God." This works at first. The rule of law is established, and nations around the world prosper as a result of fairness and justice through law. Many think that humanity finally has hope to thrive. Unfortunately, democracy, in the end, becomes a tool to unite the world under the power of the Antichrist.

What most people don't know is that Satan likes to lead the crowd. His first attempt to lead the world by the voice of the majority happened at Babel, the first human civilization. Leadership was still a strange concept for many back then, so humans of the entire planet got together and began to plan their future without an established leader. Driven by satanic power, they began to build to ensure that they remain together. Genesis 11:3-4 expresses the sense of majority rule, saying, *"**They said** to each other, 'Come, **let's make** bricks and bake them thoroughly.' ... Then **they said**, 'Come, **let us build ourselves** a city, with a tower that reaches to the heavens, so that **we may make** a name for ourselves; otherwise **we will** be scattered over the face of the whole earth"* (emphasis added). To buy humans time, God decided to divide them and scatter them over the face of the earth.

In these last days, Satan tries to do the same thing. He wants a majority rule in every nation of the planet. That's why spreading democracy around the world is so crucial before the manifestation of the Antichrist. While men celebrate peace and safety, the Word of God predicted in 1 Thessalonians 5:3 that *"destruction will come on them suddenly, as labor pains on a pregnant woman, and they will not escape."*

CONTROLLING THE WORLD WEALTH

Satan's legions also use ideas of freedom to control the world's wealth. This translates into capitalism or free market. Satan uses capitalism to create a single financial circulatory system for the world. The same way democracy makes a world government possible, capitalism makes a world economy possible. So what's wrong with a world economy? Nothing until Satan controls the world's wealth and uses it to control every aspect of human lives.

Controlling the world's wealth gives him control over the entire world. It enables him to put in or remove from leadership positions whomever he wants both in governments and in the private sector. It enables him to control the media and public opinion. By controlling the media, he is able to tell you who to vote for, what's good, what's wrong, what's cool, and what's lame. This is especially true, because humanity at this point has no God but himself. Most people on earth are in survival mode and everyone is only looking out for "self."

DESTROYING THE FAMILY

The family unit is an image of God's family. Satan hates it, because it teaches humanity about what a relationship with their Heavenly Father may look like. Therefore, at all costs, Satan seeks to change that image so that humanity will not be reminded of its origin.

God's intent was to use the family as a primary learning environment. Family builds a foundation so that individuals who have that foundation are less susceptible to moving away from it later in life. Family is the first church or synagogue. Proverb 22:6 says, *"Start children off on the way they should go, and even when they are old they will not turn from it."* In other words, the things people learn in the family environment when they are still young will be remembered and will shape their beliefs when they grow up.

Satan, on the other hand, prefers free agents, because they are easily persuaded. He likes people who have no foundation, and because they lack a clear path, they can easily be programmed to follow him. Therefore, Satan must destroy the primary source of fundamentalism by sending his legions out into the world to destroy the family structure.

To accelerate the destruction of the family, which sin already started to do, Satan used the emancipation of women. Again, because most people don't know the end, the emancipation of women sounds very appealing at first, but in the end, it is the tool that kills family. Adam was created perfect with no weaknesses until he desired a helper. Eve became his only weakness, and Satan used her to take down Adam and the whole creation with him. Because men are spiritually and naturally equipped to lead the family, removing that leadership will have disastrous consequences. Therefore, Satan decided to repeat what he did in the Garden of Eden. He promoted women's leadership.

The biblical family structure is defined through the relationship between Christ and the church. Paul, on multiple occasions, compared Adam to Christ. In a few other places, he compared the husband to Christ and the wife to the church. Therefore, there is little or no argument that Christ and the church are a model of marriage.

In God's family model, Christ is not equal to the church. He is above the church. He does not just occupy a superior position as Lord, but He is the visionary of the unit. In other words, Christ decides what direction the family takes. Get ready to be offended! Christ and the church don't make unanimous decisions. Christ is to be followed. Any ambitions the church might have ought to be approved by Christ, otherwise the church falls out of God's will, and so do wives when they do not submit to their husbands.

A FEMINIST APPROACH TO THE WORD OF GOD

In the final age, Satan successfully conditions women believers to look at the Word of God through a feminist lens. Many of those who preach the Gospel are promoting women in power and omit or change the Word of God as they do so. Women preachers who do not attempt to reinterpret the biblical command of *"wives, submit to your own husbands, as to the Lord"* (Ephesians 5:22) are a rarity. The notion of submission is just foreign in the final condition, not just for women, but for the majority of the world.

During the final age, Christians still believe they have a spirit, soul, and body. However, conditioning sneaks up on them. They believe that they are spiritual beings living in physical bodies, but their hearts are thorny ground so that many of them are compromised. Social transformation, triggered by the "freedom campaign," influences how they view not only the world, but also the Word of God.

Progressivism affects the church so much so that the last generation of Christians no longer believe in the biblical hierarchy of family. Those who confess to still believe in the biblical family structure either never preach it or they compromise it when they preach it. Women are the most affected, because many have been raised to believe in the Bible, but due to conditioning, they secretly think the Word of God is unfair toward women. Therefore, they relate to parts of God's Word that does not go against their feminist views, and are very uncomfortable when anyone touches the Bible's perspective on women's role in a family setting.

Because of feminism, many Bible scholars would rather preach "equality" instead of the biblical "submission" model of the marriage structure. Why would anyone want to submit to anyone? Often, when preachers get to this point, they compromise the authority of the Word of God by trying to be fair. Therefore, they feel obligated to also emphasize the Scripture that says, *"Let the husband render to his wife the affection due her"* (1 Corinthians 7:3).

CONCLUSION

The foundation of a believer is the Word of God. True believers don't seek their own private interpretation of the Word of God, but they desire that the Word of God would speak for itself. They hunger to know what the spirit of the Word is trying to communicate to them.

However, when people no longer believe in the Word, they desire a word that agrees with their views and opinions. They no longer trust in the perfect divine wisdom. The Word of God is no longer a mirror in which to find what needs fixing in their lives, but instead becomes their own masterpiece painting. The look into the Word, not for it to tell them how they look, but for them to paint their own pictures into the Word.

Two thousand years ago, Jesus foresaw the Age of the Gods (see chapter 6) and noticed how many believers were worried that the world was growing hostile toward the Bible, believers, Israel, and God Himself. Hence, knowing that many in such difficult times would be reading the Bible, He sent a message to his followers into the future, saying, *"Heaven and earth will pass away, but My words will by no means pass away"* (Matthew 24:35). His message is not a sign of desperation, but confidence in the sovereignty of His Word. While many are compromising to fit into a new world, even *"the gates of Hades shall not prevail against"* (Matthew 16:18) those who truly seek Him.

CHAPTER 8

THE FIVE GATES OF HEAVEN

TRUE SALVATION

DECOY SALVATION

Because of conditioning, many of those who are preaching salvation are preaching a decoy salvation. Those who believe in the decoy salvation think they are saved, but they've never truly been saved. These are counted among those that the Lord Jesus tells in the end, *"I never knew you."*

The decoy salvation message takes advantage of people's new ability to strongly believe in their own opinions. They cannot be convinced of their sins, because they've been trained to only have a positive attitude about self. Therefore, decoy salvation preachers avoid touching on self by presenting a "restoration" story instead of a "reconciliation-restoration" story.

These preachers avoid showing that the very need for humanity to be saved is because of sin. Instead, they present social problems as the reason why people need Christ. The decoy salvation message tends to omit humanity's responsibility for its condition.

With no guilt there is no asking for forgiveness. Therefore, those who are exposed to the decoy salvation message do not use the Word of God to measure whether they are saved or not, but they convince themselves that they are saved without any true reconciliation with God. In other words, they want the reward of reconciliation without reconciling.

DECOY FORGIVENESS

The Holy Spirit's voice that convinces of sin is buried in the surrounding noise of self-building words. Satan's message in the world is "no guilt, enjoy life." Therefore, you hear this message everywhere: in movies, on television shows, in books, and even in churches.

In fact, this message is the new tone of the Gospel around the world. Instead of *"repentance and remission of sins,"* according to Luke 24:46–47, Gospel preachers are preaching only *"remission of sins"* and calling unrepenting believers to benefit from the rewards of repentance. Salvation without repentance is easy and appealing to the world. Consequently, churches that carry this kind of message are filled with people.

Those who genuinely seek salvation have a hard time identifying the voice of God under such conditions. They wonder if the voice of the Holy Spirit is the voice that calls them to "repent and believe" or the voice that tells them to "believe and enjoy" their earthly lives. Both messages are being preached by people who claim to be from God, but for the many the "believing and enjoying" philosophy is more appealing.

Satan understands that without true repentance reconciliation is not possible. Therefore, he launches a war against the voice that "[convicts] *the world of sin...of righteousness, and of judgment*" (John 16:8). As long as people are not listening to this voice, they cannot be convinced they are sinners, righteous, or judged.

INDUCED GUILT RESISTANT

The message of repentance is what triggers "conviction of sin." Therefore, Satan launches a war against it. He bombards the world with teachings and entertainment that convey "positive thinking" messages so that many people become guilt resistant. Society perceives "feeling guilty" as a psychological disease rather than an important component of humanity's ability to self-evaluate. Without such an ability, humans turn into psychopathic beings who cannot feel remorse after sinning against God.

CAN HUMAN BEINGS BE RIGHTEOUS?

The message of righteousness is what triggers the belief that humanity can become righteous. Therefore, Satan launches a war against believing in "righteousness." First, he bombards believers with an overstated message of grace so that they become comfortable with sin. Second, he bombards both believers and nonbelievers with an overstated message of the "fallen condition" so that many embrace the idea that "humanity is corrupt and can never be righteous."

Sin becomes accepted as a part of human nature, and churches no longer preach on repentance and forgiveness of sins. Therefore, it becomes accepted that to live happy lives, human beings must not try to contain sinful urges. Instead, they must be unleashed as long as they do not harm anyone.

Consequently, the mindset of living for pleasure enters denominations. Divorce is never an option, but suddenly it becomes an option. Homosexuality is a sin, but suddenly pulpits are open to homosexuals. It becomes accepted that God understands that we can't resist our own nature, so He automatically overlooks the sinful results of our nature. To describe this way of thinking, the Apostle Paul states that people have become "*lovers of pleasure rather than lovers of God*" (2 Timothy 3:5). Because they love pleasure more than they love God, they even ask God in prayer whether they should break one of the ten commandments or not.

- Can I enter my third marriage, Lord?
- Can I divorce my drunk husband?
- Because we are meant to be together, can we divorce our current spouses and get married, Lord? We just want to know Your will.

SALVATION

Anyone who has had a real encounter with Jesus Christ of the Bible goes through five gates to enter the salvation Jesus Christ offers at Calvary. To be saved, you must enter:

1. **Repentance**: It is the first step of salvation, nothing else happens without it.

2. **Reconciliation**: By the power of the Holy Spirit, the Lord Jesus Christ takes you through this gate and reconciles you with God so that God can accept you as His son or daughter.

3. **Redemption**: At this point, the Devil still has a claim over you as his slave and captive. Therefore, Jesus Christ takes you through this gate to wash you in His blood and to mark you as a redeemed.

4. **Rebirth**: Then the newly redeemed soul is handed over to the Holy Ghost who

turns it into a new soul, born of a seed of righteousness.

5. **Regeneration**: Finally, as it happens naturally, the Holy Ghost also triggers a never-ending process of regeneration that results in growth, tissue repairs (scarring), and spiritual development in general.

The five gates are entered in the above order. There are no shortcuts which allows one to skip a gate or choose a different starting gate. To be saved through Jesus Christ, everyone, living or dead, must go through these phases. Why then are the five gates relevant in the context of this book?

The Devil understands this process better than most believers. By trial and error and over a period of 2000 years, he has learned what strategies against the Gospel are the most efficient. He knows persecution doesn't work well. He knows that false doctrine does work. However, when a new revival breaks out, the body of Christ recovers in a spectacular way.

Therefore, his new strategy is try to influence how new "born-again" believers are conceived. Ideally, he doesn't even want conception to happen, but if it happens, his goal is to cause an abortion. He accomplishes this through compromise. Many preachers of the Gospel are so caught up into trying to be accepted that they completely erase repentance from the Gospel.

As a result, salvation becomes an illusion to the point where many believe they are saved, but their salvation process has never even started.

REPENTANCE

In these days, most people don't know that they are lost to sin. Satan turns the world against the very need for salvation by bringing deceptive teachings. As previously mentioned, he brings a decoy salvation message such that people think they need to be saved from hunger, illnesses, or poverty. Moreover, he spreads teachings that induce guilt resistance, presenting guilt as only a negative satanic influence so that people rarely think of guilt as the voice of the Holy Ghost "[convicting them] *of sin, and of righteousness, and of judgment*" (John 16:8).

The online Merriam-Webster's dictionary defines repentance as *"the action or process of repenting especially for misdeeds or moral shortcomings."* So other than being a biblical teaching, repentance is common in society. Whenever people recognize their wrongdoings toward one another, regret their actions, and hope they could take them back, they've already repented. In fact, true repentance always occurs inside the heart before an action is taken to repair the damages the offense caused.

Satan's goal is to prevent people from reaching salvation. Because of that, one of his strategies is to suppress repentance from the path of those who are getting closer to salvation. To accomplish this, he simply generates a phobia for the biblical Gospel, replacing it with teachings that are based on social wisdom. The Apostle Peter stated in 2 Peter 3:9, *"The Lord is not slack concerning His promise, as some count slackness, but is longsuffering toward us, not willing that any should perish but that all should come to repentance."* This statement by the Apostle Peter implies that in order for humanity not to "perish" they must "come to repentance."

Therefore, to even consider reconciliation with God a possibility, one must first repent. This is also true in human society. Imagine a person who offends you and then pretends it never happened. Just as common social wisdom expects true repentance in order to grant forgiveness, all God requires from us, in order for Him to freely give us salvation, is repentance—an infinitely smaller price compared to the price He paid for our salvation.

Unfortunately, since the world can never truly live guilt-free, the last world is conditioned to live guilt resistant. Every voice in society is saying:

- You are only human.
- Don't be hard on yourself.
- If God is loving, He should understand human weaknesses.
- And many other such concepts.

RECONCILIATION

In our society, when one asks for forgiveness, you get two types of reactions from the guilty party. When the guilty party is truly repenting, you often see a persistent effort to show regret and a desire to repair the wrong. When the guilty party is not repenting, you often get an insincere apology, such as: "What's the big deal? I've already said sorry." Out of these two types of individuals, who do you think is more likely to be forgiven? Salvation is a reconciliation story. How can we reconcile an offender with the person they offended by skipping repentance?

Many in the last days come to the kingdom with the "What's the big deal!" attitude. Often, the attitude is fueled by very accommodating gospels that confuse "commit all you want" with "come as you are." Jesus comes for sinners because He wants to heal them from humanity's one and only problem—sin. Unfortunately, in the end, very few find salvation because reconciling with God only matters to very few. The few who are saved are the ones who, not only accept the gift from God, but they are also willing to fight the *"good fight of faith"* (1 Timothy 6:12).

The whole salvation story is about reconciliation. However, in the Age of the Gods, the effect of conditioning on the church changes salvation into only a deliverance story. People can be delivered from illnesses, poverty, and many other bondages or oppressions that humanity suffers and end up in hell, but you can never end up in hell when you are reconciled with God. That is why it is so important for Satan to get people as far from repentance as possible. Because that's where reconciliation with God starts.

- We are called to reconcile the world with God: *"Now all things are of God, who has reconciled us to Himself through Jesus Christ, and has given us the ministry of reconciliation"* (2 Corinthians 5:18).
- Reconciliation is a condition for salvation: *"For if when we were enemies we were reconciled to God through the death of His Son, much more, having been reconciled, we shall be saved by His life"* (Romans 5:10).

REDEMPTION

Because people living in the end of the world are conditioned to not to see the need for reconciliation with God, many never make it to the redemption gate. Those who make it here are the ones who successfully cause *"joy in heaven over one sinner who repents"* (Luke 15:7). At this point, God makes the blood of Jesus available to redeem them from eternal condemnation. The majority of those who claim to be saved don't make it here, because they were never repenting souls and, consequently, were never reconciled with God.

All men without Christ are sinners and condemned. This is a fact that no liberal propaganda, television or secular scientist's mockeries can ever change. Two thousand years ago, nobody had proof that the earth was round, but that did not change the fact that it was. If you were to try to save Sodom and Gomorrah, the only chance you would have is to convince the people of both cities to repent and ask for God's mercy.

All have sinned and fall short of the glory of God, being justified freely by His grace through the redemption that is in Christ Jesus. – Romans 3:23–24

The online Merriam-Webster's dictionary defines redemption as *"the act of making something better or more acceptable or the act of exchanging something for money, an award, etc."* When repenting and reconciled sinners reach the redemption gate, the blood of Jesus Christ washes them, their sins are forgiven, their prison bailout is paid, and their criminal record deleted.

Who gave Himself for us, that He might redeem us from every lawless deed and purify for Himself His own special people, zealous for good works. – Titus 2:14

REBIRTH

One of Merriam-Webster's definitions of rebirth is *"a period of new life, growth, or activity."* In the same sense, once the repented and reconciled souls are redeemed, they move to the fourth "R-Gate"—rebirth. They must start a new life, because the old nature is corrupt and cannot see God. Therefore, they are handed over to the Holy Spirit, who not only plants a seed of the new life in them, but also nurtures and watches over the growing seed.

Under the control of the Spirit of God, when the seed completes the gestation period, rebirth takes place, and all the souls that entered the rebirth gate become new a creation. *"Old things have passed away; behold, all things have become new"* (2 Corinthians 5:17). How long the gestation period takes is a mystery that only God knows.

Jesus Christ tries to explain the rebirth to Nicodemus in John chapter 3 saying, *"Most assuredly, I say to you, unless one is born again, he cannot see the kingdom of God."* Clearly only believers who are able to go through the rebirth gate may enter the Kingdom of God.

To explain rebirth, Peter wrote, *"Having been born again, not of corruptible seed but incorruptible, through the word of God which lives and abides forever."* This means that the seed we receive is actually the Word of God. So in some sense, we are born of the Word of God. The Word of God is the spiritual makeup of a born-again believer. In fact, Jesus Himself states that *"unless one is born of water and the Spirit, he cannot enter the kingdom of God"* (John 3:5). In Holy Scriptures, water is often a symbol of the Word (see John 4:1–26).

Many of Satan's activities during humanity's last

condition are concentrated on rebirth. Even biologically, from seeding to birth, many things can happen. Satan knows that once rebirth candidates are born-again, it is almost impossible to take them out of the path toward the Kingdom of God. Therefore, his goal is to stop rebirth.

Many people reach the rebirth gate, but very few actually go through it. Due to the conditioning of the denominational church, many get aborted or die before rebirth due to the lack of adequate spiritual nourishment. Some reach rebirth, but with developmental problems. Remember, we are born of the Word of God, and unfortunately, denominations, during the last conditioning period, have become infected, and the word they preach is infected with substances that ultimately cause spiritual death or spiritual retardation.

That's why, compared to the church where truth is still being preached, the conditioned church is filled with people, but most of them are either spiritual zombies or spiritually retarded. Here are some of things that characterize them:

- A strong lack of interest in reading and knowing the Word of God.
- A strong resemblance to the world.
- A strong desire to remain connected to and live like the world.

- A strong tendency to live for and desire what the world desires. The only difference between them and the world is that they believe God is the one who helps them fulfill their desires.

- The world's views and opinions strongly affect how they interpret the Word of God.

- They only do spiritual things that they enjoy in the flesh.

- They can be going to church for years, but never grow in their service to and knowledge of God.

- They are very opinionated because they consider themselves open minded, and because of that, they have an attitude that resists discipleship (can't follow the minister or servant God establishes over them because they are conditioned not to trust spiritual leaders).

On the other hand, those who go through rebirth become a new creation. The nature of God is now slowly growing in them. Just like children are attached to their mothers, they are very attached to the things of God and are hungry for the knowledge of the Word. Here are some of the traits you find in truly born-again believers:

- They love the Word of God.

- They lack a desire to resemble to the world, so they speak, dress, and behave differently.
- The primary driver for their faith is their determination to enter the Kingdom of God and be reunited with their heavenly Father.
- Their spiritual growth is fast and noticeable to the world.
- They are uncomfortable around worldly people and worldly people are uncomfortable around them.
- They are the happiest when doing spiritual things such as praying or worshiping.
- They trust in the will of God for their lives and believe it is the best thing that can happen to them, regardless of what it is.
- They strive to live a holy life, because they know that their bodies are temples of the Holy Spirit. Indeed, they also know that they have given their lives to God as an offering.

REGENERATION

Regeneration is nothing other than growth and maintenance of the new lives those who experience rebirth acquire. The best illustration of regeneration is natural regeneration. Natural regeneration and spiritual regeneration are very much alike.

Physiologically, the phenomenon that is responsible for the development of a child in a mother's womb is also responsible for regeneration once the child is born or during the child's lifetime. Biologists call it "cell division." We experience regeneration every day. In fact, natural regeneration is a constant process. Our bodies almost constantly lose cells, and these are being constantly replaced by newer and younger cells. The most common example of regeneration in humans is cicatrization, which is defined as "scar formation at the site of a healing wound" (*Merriam-Webster's online dictionary*).

Regeneration officially starts once all the organs of a fetus are fully developed in the womb. That is because any cell division that occurs prior to that is considered part of the fetus development process. Once the organs are functional and fully developed, cell division takes on an additional function, which is maintenance. The newly formed organs not only need to continue to grow, but they also need to heal when necessary. Therefore, "cell division" continues until we die.

In the same manner, the phenomenon responsible for spiritual rebirth is also responsible for regeneration. Paul writes to Titus saying that *"not by works of righteousness which we have done, but according to His mercy He saved us, through the washing of regeneration and renewing of the Holy Spirit"* (Titus 3:5). Clearly, the power of the Holy Spirit in reborn believers is responsible for regeneration.

Unfortunately, just like in our natural lives, certain factors can prevent regeneration. For example, a wound may get infected so that parasites begin to make it worse. Spiritually, there can also be parasites in our lives. These are things or people that negatively affect our spiritual growth. It could be as simple as a new friend who drives you away from church or an activity that prevents you from spending time with God in prayer and His Word. Jesus said, *"If your hand or foot causes you to sin, cut it off and cast it from you. It is better for you to enter into life lame or maimed, rather than having two hands or two feet, to be cast into the everlasting fire"* (Matthew 18:8). Here Jesus is talking about spiritual parasites. Satan sends them in a believer's life to hinder spiritual development of growth.

Spiritual regeneration is a set of things performed by both the Holy Spirit and the believer to maintain the new creation. As a way to regenerate the believer's mind so that it differs from a worldly mind, Paul said, *"Do not be conformed to this world, but be transformed by the renewing of your mind, that you may prove what is that good and acceptable and perfect will of God"* (Romans 12:1–2). In other words, a born-again believer always tries to conform to the Word of God instead of conforming to the world, and this tendency allows the renewing of the mind so that we become convinced of what the perfect will of God is.

CONCLUSION

Regardless of conditioning, true believers continue to hunger for God. In fact, the end-time world condition makes them desire the Kingdom of God more. Although conditioning affects many of them to some extent, it ultimately becomes the main reason why they hunger for the rapture more than any other generation before them.

Those who have Christ do not fear powers that are operating in this world. Just as Jesus Christ turned down Satan's offer for world dominion at the cost of worshiping him (Matthew 4:1–11), last-days believers will turn down Satan's propositions in all their forms. These believers will become so hated by the world that a remnant is forced to become a secret society in order to keep the faith.

Beware of conditioned preachers. They are mercenaries and have no intention of leading anyone into the Kingdom of Heaven. Not only do they lack discernment as to what season we are in, but they are incapable of reading the divine clock. Jesus worries about them from the beginning and says in Matthew 24:45, *"Who then is a faithful and wise servant, whom his master made ruler over his household, to give them food in due season?"* There is food; the question is whether there is a "wise servant" to give it during a season when God's people need it the most.

Although Satan successfully conditions millions to

rebel against God, in the end, the Word of God comes to pass, and Christ establishes His eternal Kingdom, restoring His nation of Israel and also saving those who love Him from the schemes of Satan. Always remember: *"Heaven and earth will pass away, but My words will by no means pass away"* (Matthew 24:35).